D1546836

P T boats

Bryan Cooper

BB

Editor-in-Chief: Barrie Pitt
Art Director: Peter Dunbar

Military Consultant: Sir Basil Liddell Hart
Picture Editor: Robert Hunt

Executive Editor: David Mason
Designer: Sarah Kingham
Special Drawings: John Batchelor
Cartographer: Richard Natkiel
Cover: Denis Piper
Research Assistant: Yvonne Marsh

Photographs for this book were especially selected from the following Archives: from left to right page 2-3 Vosper-Thornycroft Ltd; 7 Vosper; 8-9 Vosper; 10 from *Alarm-Schnellboote*; 11 US Navy; 12-13 Imperial War Museum; 13 IWM; 14 Vosper; 15 Vosper; 16-17 from *Alarm-Schnellboote*; 18-19 Vosper; 22-23 IWM; 26 Vosper; 26-27 from *Alarm-Schnellboote*; 28-29 IWM; 32 Vosper; 33 Vosper; 34 IWM; 35 Vosper; 36-37 IWM; 38-39 Vosper; 40-41 IWM; 43 IWM; 44 IWM; 45 from *Flag 4*; 46-47 Vosper; 48-49 IWM; 51 IWM; 52 from *The Battle of the Narrow Seas*; 53 from *The Battle of the Narrow Seas*; 56 IWM; 57 Bibliothek fur Zeitgeschichte; 60 IWM; 62-63 Vosper; 64 IWM/from *Alarm-Schnellboote*; 65 IWM; 68 from *Alarm-Schnellboote*; 69 from *Alarm-Schnellboote*; 70-71 IWM; 72 Vosper; 73 Vosper; 74 IWM/Vosper; 75 IWM/Vosper; 76 IWM; 76-77 IWM; 77 Vosper; 78-79 Ullstein; 80-81 US Navy; 86 US Navy; 90-91 IWM; 92 IWM; 93 IWM; 96 IWM/from *Flag 4*; 99 US Navy/from *Flag 4*; 100 IWM; 107 from *Flag 4*; 108-109 from *Flag 4*; 110-111 IWM; 112 from *Die Deutsche Kriegsmarine im Kampf 1939-1945*; 112-113 IWM; 115 IWM; 116-117 IWM; 118-119 IWM; 120-121 IWM; 124 US Navy; 127 US Navy; 130 US Navy; 132-133 US Navy; 134-135 US Navy; 135 US Navy; 136 US Navy; 137 US Navy; 138-139 US Navy; 140-141 US Navy; 142 US Navy; 143 US Navy; 152-153 Vosper; 154-155 Vosper; 156-157 Vosper

First printing: June 1970
Printed in United States of America

Ballantine Books Inc.
101 Fifth Avenue New York NY 10003

Contents

Sea heritage

Introduction by David Mason

In introducing a book about small ships by an English author, an English commentator might perhaps be permitted a certain feeling of patriotic pride, in view of the traditional image we British cherish so dearly of a seafaring nation with salt-water coursing in our veins.

In fact such patriotism and pride are somewhat misplaced, for two reasons. One is the obvious injustice of partisanship, for there is no doubt that other nations have equally important seafaring traditions which found expression in the use of small boats during the war. The second is that despite their tradition, the British had during the inter-war years neglected with almost fatal results the importance of small boats in future hostilities. Having built up a force of coastal motor boats and motor launches during the First World War the British failed for fifteen years afterwards to pay any further attention to their role, and only in 1934 did the government begin to consider building up a fleet. From then on progress was no better than moderate, while the

Germans and Italians both made great strides and at the outbreak of war enjoyed considerable superiority in light craft.

Thus when the war began Britain had to rely, in this sphere as in so many others, not on the quantity of her materials but on the quality of her people, and in this there was fortunately no deficiency. When the call went out for volunteers to sail to Dunkirk to snatch the retreating British Expeditionary Force out of Continental Europe, barely trained boys from the naval training establishment near Dover volunteered in hoards and lied shamelessly about their experience in order to win a place in the fleet. Many of those boys, and most of the men who followed them into Coastal Forces, were part-time sailors of the Royal Naval Volunteer Reserve, the so-called 'wavy navy' after their wavy stripes of rank, contrasted with the straight stripes worn by career naval officers. They came from all professions and trades, and had in common only their passion for the sea and small boats, and of course

their determination to sail those boats into battle against Britain's enemies.

Typical of such men was the officer who came to be regarded as the father of Britain's Coastal Forces, Lieutenant-Commander Robert Hichens. After graduating from Oxford, he was driving home to Falmouth to become a solicitor, and on the way called in at Bristol to enquire about joining the Royal Naval Volunteer Reserve. When they imposed the impossible condition that he should travel from Falmouth to Bristol twice weekly for training, Hichens realised how many potential recruits were being lost, and actually persuaded the Admiralty to start the Royal Naval Volunteer Supplementary Reserve, so that young men could be trained in their own areas. Hichens dominated Coastal Forces until 1943, when he was killed by a stray bullet on his 148th operation. He had been in action fourteen times, had won the DSO and Bar and the DSC and two Bars, and was twice mentioned in dispatches

But enough of patriotic nostalgia!

In this Ballantine series, which is designed to be supra-national in scope, all the authors deal where appropriate with the efforts of all nations. And this Bryan Cooper has certainly done. His book ranges round all the world's coasts and describes the approach to coastal forces of all the warring nations, including Japan who alone made the mistake of ignoring this type of weapon, and paid heavily for it. He also shows that each nation had its Hichens, and that we British by no means had a monopoly of this brand of heroism, as was amply demonstrated by the activities of one of the most famous among patrol boat skippers, the late John F Kennedy.

What Bryan Cooper's admirable book shows above all is that every country would do well to heed, now and in the future as much as in the Second World War, the words of Winston Churchill to British shipyard workers in 1942: 'Without ships we cannot live and without them we cannot conquer'.

Need for little ships

The motor torpedo boat was both the smallest and fastest of the surface fighting craft to take part in the Second World War. With the advantage of a shallow draught to penetrate minefields and harbour defences, and high speed and manoeuvrability, the motor torpedo boat answered the need for a weapon that could take the war close into enemy coastal waters, specialising in sudden, unexpected attacks on coastal shipping.

It was usually at night that these craft operated, both because surprise was a major element in their attack and because by day, lightly armed as they were, they were themselves vulnerable to attack from the air and from larger warships. Speed was the essence of their success – some craft were capable of well over forty knots. But it was not so much a requirement for attack as for getting safely away afterwards. The drawback of high

Vosper 70-foot MTB taken over from the Greek navy

speed, especially at night, was the foaming wake it created, giving away a craft's presence and position. So the ideal torpedo attack was often made by lying in wait with engines cut in the path of a convoy, then moving slowly on silent auxiliary engines towards a target, launching torpedoes, and crash-starting the main engines to escape counterattack from the convoy escorts, possibly under cover of smokescreens. On occasion, when they remained unsighted even after launching their torpedoes, they might manage to slip quietly away without the enemy being aware of their presence, and the torpedo hits might then be put down to hitting mines. When they were sighted and engaged in battle, motor torpedo boats fought at closer quarters than any other naval vessels of the war.

Coastal shipping was a vital factor in every theatre of war. For Britain it was the most practical method of transferring goods and materials from the industrial north to the south, by way of the east coast routes. To a lesser extent this also applied to Germany, along the occupied coast of Western Europe on the other side of the North Sea. In the Mediterranean, the land battles in North Africa, Sicily and Italy hinged on the vital need to keep open the coastal supply lines, as important to the Allies as to the Axis powers. In the island battles of the Pacific, both the Americans and the Japanese were largely dependent on coastal shipping and barge traffic for transferring their forces from one area to another and in keeping them supplied. And it was through the coastal waters off Burma and Malaya that the Japanese brought most of the supplies to their forces in northern Burma rather than through the difficult jungle routes inland, a factor that became of major importance in the Arakan campaigns. Motor torpedo boats were used effectively in all these areas.

But their role was not limited to attacks on coastal shipping. They

Left: Camouflaged German S-boat
in the Baltic. *Above:* One of the first
Higgins PT boats

were also used defensively, sometimes
being the only craft fast enough to
combat enemy motor torpedo boats.
They played an important part in
combined operations raids, such as
that on St Nazaire, and particularly
in the Pacific campaigns by supporting
beach landings on Japanese-occupied
islands. They raided harbours, landed
secret agents on lonely enemy shores,
and in the Mediterranean developed
techniques for boarding and capturing
merchant ships in the manner of the
buccaneers of old. Their only limita-
tions were in range, because of the
high fuel consumption of their powerful engines, in vulnerability to attack
during daylight, and an inability
because of their size and somewhat
fragile construction to operate in very
heavy seas.

Motor torpedo boats spearheaded a
class of small boats that also included
motor gunboats and armed motor
launches, although in some cases, as
with the German *Schnellboote* (fast
motor torpedo boat) – in many ways
the most successful of all such craft –
a variety of functions including mine-
laying and convoy escort work as well
as torpedo attack were carried out by
the one type of boat. The American PT
(patrol torpedo) boats also combined
the roles of gunboat and torpedo
carrier. The British navy tended in the
early years of the war to separate
these two functions, developing MGBs
(motor gunboats) as distinct from
MTBs (motor torpedo boats). It was
mainly with the introduction of the
larger Fairmile 'D' boats in 1942 that
the concepts of attack by gun and
torpedo were combined in one craft.

The country that had paid most
attention to the development of motor
torpedo boats before the war was

Italy. The Italian navy entered the war with a force of over one hundred MAS (anti-submarine motor torpedo) boats, as many as all the other major powers put together. By the end of the war, however, Britain had built up the largest fleet with more than 1,500 small boats in Coastal Forces.

Conversely, the Japanese did less than any other country in developing such craft, preferring to concentrate on larger warships. Only a relatively small number of T-type motor torpedo boats were built, to the design of a British First World War Thornycroft craft captured at Canton in 1938. In the closing stages of the war, the Japanese tried to make up lost ground by build-ing large numbers of *Shinyo* boats – one-man suicide motor boats, sixteen feet long, which were loaded with explosives in their bows and intended to be driven by their pilots against enemy vessels. These had very little success – they were usually hunted out and destroyed by the American PT boats before they could be put into operation. There is no doubt that in the Pacific island campaigns, the Japanese suffered heavily by not having a suitable craft with which to combat the PT boats of the US Navy.

Motor torpedo boats were not, of course, the only weapons to be used in the struggle for command of coastal waters. Other ships were involved; the

German S-boat commanders, for instance, feared Allied destroyers more than they did the motor gunboats that had been designed specifically to be used in combat against them. But a tactical combination of the two, destroyer and MGB, was even more effective, as later operations in the North Sea proved.

Air power had an even greater role to play, certainly by day. Its value in attacking enemy warships and merchant shipping was one of the great lessons of the war. But again, it was even more successful when used in co-operation with other forces. By mid-1943, Britain's Coastal Forces were working closely with Fighter Command groups in offensive sweeps against enemy shipping between the Dutch coast and the approaches to the English Channel. This was part of the growing inter-dependence between all the various Services that became an increasing factor as the war progressed and which was the key to most defence policies of the post-war years.

There were many areas in which small craft kept up the watchful work of patrolling and seldom, if ever, came into contact with the enemy, such as

Fairmile submarine chasers on patrol. *Left:* Off Newfoundland. *Below:* Off the New Zealand coast

the Caribbean, the Aleutians, and off the coasts of West and South Africa. But in terms of offensive action, they were involved in three main areas of conflict. First, there was the fight for the narrow seas between Britain and Europe, which began with Germany's occupation of the whole seaboard of Western Europe. The North Sea and English Channel saw the greatest confrontation of the war between the motor torpedo boats as both sides strove to attack the other's coastal convoys, as well as defending their own.

Included in the Coastal Forces of Britain were crews and boats from the Dominions and the free forces of Europe and, at a later date, from America. It was not until the end of 1942 that Britain began to reach equal terms with the German S-boats (or E boats as they were generally known, standing for Enemy War Motorboat). The battle built up to a climax at the end of 1942 and again in 1944 with the Normandy landings. It lasted until the very end of the war when the German

Vosper 70-foot MTBs

boats, although by then outnumbered and outclassed, were still harrying Allied shipping.

The second area of conflict was in the Mediterranean, extending from the coastal waters of North Africa to Italy and the Balkans. Malta figured prominently in this struggle, both as a base for MTBs and a target of attack for German and Italian boats, as each side fought to keep open the lines of supply to their land forces. But as the net tightened round German-occupied Europe, especially after Italy's surrender in 1943, there was increasing scope in other areas for motor torpedo boats. Operating in the Aegean and Adriatic, they took part in Commando raids and carried out missions in co-operation with partisans behind enemy lines, hiding up by day in the quiet bays and inlets of the many islands of these regions. This kind of role, in which – either singly or in units – craft would set out to harass the enemy and sometimes be away· from their main bases for days or weeks at a time, ideally suited the individualistic temperament of those who served in small boats. American PT boats worked side by side with British and Dominion Coastal Forces. For a while, a PT squadron was the sole representative of the US Navy in these waters.

The third area in which motor torpedo boats were widely used was the Pacific. Although British Coastal Forces were employed to a limited extent off the coasts of Malaya and Burma, it was mainly the American PT boats that fought the Japanese in the island-hopping campaigns of New Guinea, the Solomon Islands, and the Philippines.

In many ways, the Pacific saw the most successful use of motor torpedo boats. The PT boats played a vital part in attacking coastal supply ships and in keeping large groups of Japanese forces bottled up in their island garrisons. In addition, they were effectively employed against enemy warships up to the size of light cruiser,

and took part in some of the most dramatic naval engagements of the Pacific war, including the Battle of Leyte Gulf.

As a fighting craft that was relatively cheap to build and simple in design, so that large numbers could be quickly

constructed even in small boatyards, the motor torpedo boat more than proved its value as a weapon during the war and underlined the importance of maintaining control of coastal waters in any conflict. But this was not the first time that the lesson had been learned, even though it might have been largely forgotten during the years between the two world wars. For, as in the case of so many modern weapons, it was in the First World War that motor torpedo boats were developed and used for the first time.

German Schnellboot at speed

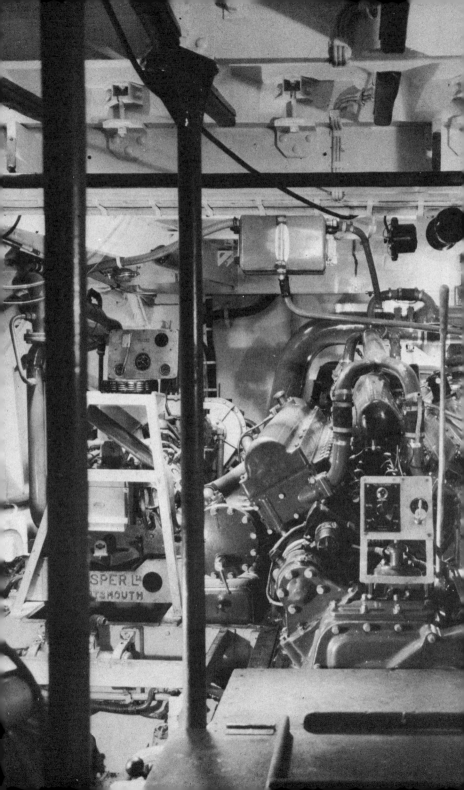

Build-up

Although motor-powered torpedo boats were initially introduced during the First World War, steam-powered craft had been in existence for some years before that. And the concept of using small boats to deliver torpedoes against enemy ships went back even further – to the days of the American Civil War.

The self-propelled torpedo was a development of the floating mine. A certain amount of confusion arose from the fact that these mines, up to the time they were first used on a large scale by the Confederate forces in the Civil War, were called torpedoes. The original invention of the floating mine is credited to an American engineer, David Bushnell. In 1775, he demonstrated that contrary to the generally held belief that the force of an underwater explosion would be dissipated through the water, such an explosion released near the hull of a ship would

Packard engine.

A spar torpedo boat of the late 1800s

in fact be driven by the pressure of the water against the hull. Even a small one of his torpedoes, as he called them, could damage a large ship. Bushnell could raise little interest in such a weapon, however, and eventually he gave up trying. Some years later another American, Robert Fulton, resurrected the idea. Since Britain and France were then at war – a war in which fighting at sea played an important part – he felt the time had come when naval powers would appreciate the value of the mine. With a fine degree of neutrality he approached first the French and then the British, proving the invention by blowing up obsolete ships during demonstrations before invited audiences of military leaders.

But beyond expressing mild interest, neither country would support the development of such a weapon. It was not only a reaction against something new and revolutionary that contradicted all previously held theories, as Bushnell had found. It was a realisation that at one stroke the mine would make vulnerable the large warships of

the day on which such countries base their power. They were not going to support such a self-defeating weapon which at the same time was considered too barbaric for civilised use.

Fulton went much further than Bushnell in developing the idea. Seeing the need also to be able to deliver explosive charges against targets, as well as using mines defensively to protect harbours from raiding ships he also invented the first crude submarine, which he called a plunging boat. This was the first conception of the torpedo as a weapon, as distinct from the floating mine. And although Fulton suffered much the same fate as Bushnell in his failure to obtain financial support for continuing his research, it was largely on his ideas that the Confederate forces based their use of mines during the American Civil War, when they employed them to some effect against blockading Union ships.

It was a Confederate officer, Captain Hunter Davidson, who developed what might be called the first torpedo boat. Whereas Fulton had thought in terms of underwater craft to deliver his torpedoes, Davidson, in 1864, hit on the

evice of fixing an explosive charge to
he end of a long pole jutting out from
he bows of a rowing boat, then setting
ff at night close to an enemy vessel
nd ramming the pole against its hull.
'his proved to be remarkably effective,
rith the one major drawback that
eing so close to the explosion, the
ttackers were often blown up together
rith those they attacked. But David-
on himself survived, and after the
rar was employed by the Argentine
overnment to organise their mine
efences.

The mine was now generally accepted
s a weapon, as countries came to see
ow effective it could be as a means of
oastal defence. In 1872 the British
hipyard of Alfred Yarrow mounted a
avidson-type spar torpedo on the
ows of a thirty-foot steam launch,
hus originating the first power-driven
orpedo boat. At about the same time
n Austrian frigate captain, Giovanni
uppis, was experimenting with
nother kind of torpedo boat, self-
ropelled by a clockwork motor, which
ould be steered and the torpedo
eleased by remote cable control from
nother boat. He took the idea to an
nglish engineer, Robert Whitehead,
ho was then managing an engine
uilding firm at Fiume in Yugoslavia.
Vhitehead rejected it as impractical,
nd instead turned his attention to the
ossibility of an explosive charge that
ould travel through the water under
s own power. When completed in 1877
his device, driven by compressed air,
ecame the first self-propelled torpedo,
he weapon that was to revolutionise
varfare at sea.

The advantages of combining the
elf-propelled torpedo with a power-
riven boat were immediately ap-
arent. Within months all the fleets
f the world were clamouring for
orpedo boats, especially the smaller
avies who saw in them an effective
nd relatively cheap weapon that
ould counter the armoured warships
f their more powerful neighbours.
he larger navies, in their turn,
ecame alarmed at the growth in the
number of torpedo boats that could
threaten their big but slower ships.
The British Admiralty was particularly concerned, and developed the
torpedo gunboat as a counter to the
torpedo boat. The gunboat proved
too slow for this purpose, however,
and so in 1892 a smaller, faster craft
was designed and built by Alfred
Yarrow as a torpedo boat destroyer.
This craft, Hornet, was the first of a
new class of warship – the destroyer.

During the First World War the
torpedo came of age as a weapon,
particularly with the development of
the submarine. As the nations armed
in the pre-war years, it became a race
for supremacy in speed and armament
between craft designed as torpedo
boats and others designed to combat
them. In fact, since destroyers themselves carried torpedoes, there was
effectively little difference between
them. Each type became steadily
bigger, so that what had begun as small
torpedo-carrying steam launches developed into ships of 1,000 tons and
more. Their very size created new
problems, both because they were
easier targets to hit and because of
their vulnerability to mines. There
was still a need, although it was little
appreciated at the time, for a small
torpedo-carrying craft of the kind
originally intended.

It was the development of the
internal combustion engine that made
the motor torpedo boat possible. The
first motor launches were built soon
after the turn of the century, mostly
in Britain, America, and Italy, and it
was not long before experiments were
being made in fitting them with
torpedoes, just as they had been fitted
to steam-driven launches. One such
boat was a forty-foot craft built in
Britain by John I Thornycroft. It was
fitted with a single torpedo, but tests
showed that when this was fired it
tended to make the boat unstable. So
a second torpedo was later added to
give balance. This was the prototype
of the 35·5-knot Thornycroft coastal
motor boat (CMB), which first came

into service with the Royal Navy in 1916, originally forty feet in length but later increased to fifty-five feet.

During that same year, the Italians also brought a number of motor torpedo boats into service, known as MAS-boats (first standing for *Motoscafo Armato SVAN*, after the yard that built them, and later, *Motoscafo Anti-Sommergibile* – motor anti-submarine boats). These boats, between fifty and sixty-nine feet long, carrying two or four torpedoes, with a top speed of thirty-three knots, were used very effectively against Austrian naval units and shipping in Adriatic harbours. Their most resounding successes were the sinking of the light cruiser *Wien* at Trieste on 9th December 1917, and the battleship *Szent Istvan* in the Straits of Otranto on 8th June 1918.

The British CMBs, of which sixty-six were brought into commission, also saw valuable service, notably in actions off the Belgian coast and during the daring raids on Zeebrugge and Ostend when amongst the many awards for gallantry won by their crews were three Victoria Crosses. But their most spectacular success came during an operation after the war. In a raid on Kronstadt in 1919 after the Russian revolution, they sank the cruiser *Oleg* and disabled two capital ships and two destroyers for the loss of only one motor torpedo boat.

Another type of small craft used by the Royal Navy which was also to play an important part during the Second World War was the motor launch (ML). Specially designed and built for the Royal Navy by the Electric Boat Company (Elco) of Connecticut, these seventy-five and eighty-foot craft were shipped across the Atlantic and first came into service in 1916. They

ere powered by two 250 horse-power
etrol engines which gave a speed of
wenty knots and were armed with
uick-firing guns. Over 500 were pur-
hased, and they proved their worth in
variety of tasks – chasing sub-
narines, escorting shipping, sweeping
p and destroying mines, laying
mokescreens, and rescuing pilots
hose aircraft had crashed into the
ea. Although they were more sea-
orthy than had first been thought,
hey were not found to be suitable for
arrying torpedoes.

In spite of the work done in America
n the Elco boats and a few experi-
nental torpedo boats built to a Lewis
ixon design that had been sold to
ussia in 1908, the US Navy saw little
eed for small boats during the First
orld War. Tentative designs for
15-foot and 150-foot craft were drawn
p for possible use in coastal defence,
ut were never built. Like the

Germans, who also neglected the
development of motor torpedo boats
although they had much more reason
to need such craft to protect their
coastline, the Americans concentrated
their efforts on building seagoing
torpedo boats and destroyers.

The successes achieved by motor
torpedo boats by no means led to their
ready acceptance by all naval planners.
Accustomed to thinking primarily in
terms of big ships, many senior officers
regarded them with a certain dis-
favour, especially as they were crewed
in the main by amateur sailors of the
volunteer reserves. Something of this
attitude remained up to and even
during the Second World War, when
Britain's Coastal Forces, for instance,
were dubbed by some 'costly farces'. It
was partly responsible for the lack of
official interest in motor torpedo
boats, both in Britain and America,
that existed between the wars. The
work in design and development that
did take place was carried out mostly
by motor boat enthusiasts like
Commander Peter du Cane and Hubert
Scott-Paine, who had the foresight to
appreciate the importance of small
craft in coastal waters.

Having scrapped or sold most of the
First World War CMBs, it was not
until 1935 that the British Admiralty
placed its first order for MTBs, as the
craft were now called. These were for
a sixty-foot hard chine planing craft
designed by Scott-Paine's British
Power Boat Company. Powered by
three 500 horse-power Napier petrol
engines giving up to thirty-three
knots and armed with two 18-inch
torpedoes and .303 machine-guns fore
and aft, these craft had a lasting
influence on all the British and
American boats built in the Second
World War. They were the first of the
modern motor torpedo boats. The
Admiralty purchased six to begin
with, which were formed into the 1st
MTB Flotilla under Lieutenant-Com-

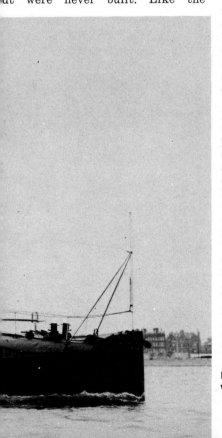

**British torpedo boat of the First
World War**

23

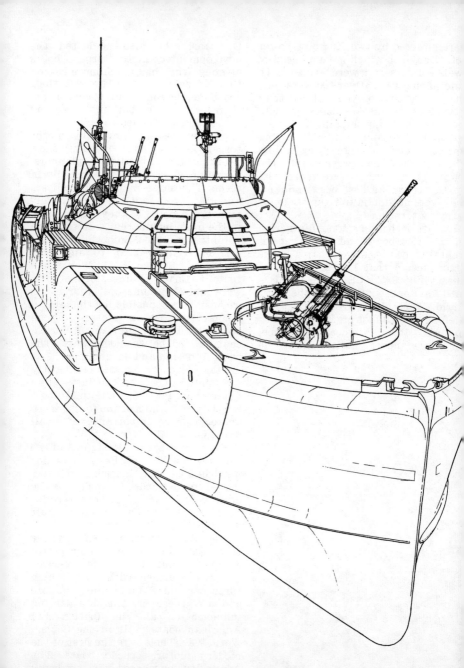

German Schnellboot
Displacement: 105 tons. *Dimensions:* 115 feet by 16¾ feet. *Crew:* 23. *Engine:* Three diesels, 7,500bhp. *Speed:* 42 knots. *Armament:* Two enclosed 21-inch torpedo tubes, one 20mm forward, one twin 20mm anti-aircraft gun, and one 37mm

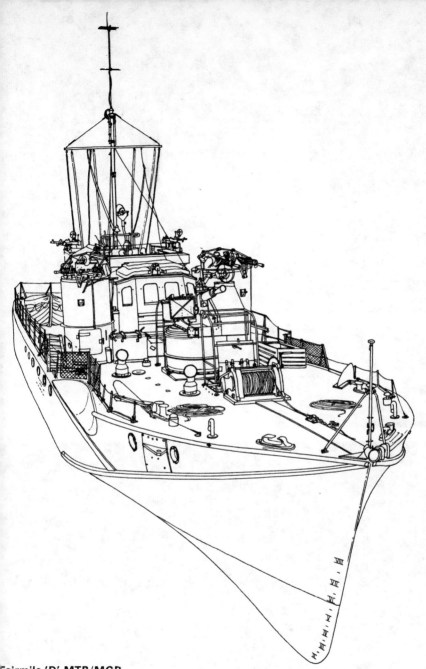

Fairmile 'D' MTB/MGB
Displacement: 90 tons (as MGB), 95 tons (as MTB), 105 tons (as combined MTB/MGB) *Dimensions:* 115 feet by 21¼ feet. *Engine:* Four Packard petrol motors, 5,000bhp. *Speed:* 27/31 knots. *Armament* Varied, but later craft had four 18-inch torpedo tubes, two 6-pounders, one twin 20mm, two twin 0.5-inch, and two twin 0.303-inch machine guns

mander G B Sayer RN, and sent to Malta in 1937.

The only official development that had taken place in America up to this time was the purchase in 1920 of two Thornycroft CMBs by the US Navy for experimental purposes. Very little official research was carried out in fact. But experiments with this type of craft were carried out in another and unexpected quarter – by the rum-runners of the Prohibition era. These men had brought in a number of the former Royal Navy craft for use in smuggling liquor from Canada to the eastern seaboard of the United States. They were constantly trying to improve the performance of the craft in order to elude the Customs patrol boats, and their experiments, which included the adaptation of the Liberty engine to marine use, provided valuable information at the beginning of the war when the US Navy first began

Divergent designs for planing hulls. *Left:* British and American boats were built of wood. *Below:* The Germans used light metal frames for their round bilge hulls

to build motor torpedo boats.

In the year that the British MTBs came into service, President Roosevelt, who as Assistant Secretary of the US Navy during the First World War had been among the few to appreciate the value of motor torpedo boats, sponsored an appropriation of $15 million for the development of suitable American small boats. In the following year, 1938, the US Navy offered prizes to private designers for a number of small boat designs, including fifty-four-foot and seventy-foot PT boats. As a result of this competition, Higgins Industries of New Orleans were given a contract in May 1939 to build two PTs, scaled up to eighty-one feet, while the US Navy itself began to build several experimental craft.

But it was in Italy that most of the early development work on motor torpedo boats was carried out, so that by the time Italy entered the war in 1940 she had more than one hundred craft in service. Most of these boats were between forty-eight and sixty feet, somewhat smaller than their British, American and German counterparts, having been designed for use in the calmer waters of the Mediterranean and Adriatic rather than, for instance, the North Sea. But they were also the fastest craft in the world at that time, powered by the excellent Isotta Fraschini marine petrol engine which gave speeds of up to forty-two knots.

Even the earliest Italian boats of the post-war period had speeds of up to forty knots. The first was built in 1929 by the SVAN yard in Venice. This was MAS 423, a forty-eight-foot craft, armed with two 6.5mm machine-guns and carrying two 17.7-inch torpedoes. Then in 1936 the Baglietto yard built a larger craft, MAS 502, which was over fifty feet in length, powered by two Isotta Fraschini engines which gave over forty-two knots, armed with one 13.2mm machine-gun, two 17.7-inch torpedoes, and six depth charges for anti-submarine operations. This became the basic design for the boats built up until 1941 which formed the bulk of the Italian motor torpedo boat fleet at that time.

The MAS-boats, although extremely fast and ideally suited for operations in shallow waters, were severely limited in their capacity to withstand heavy seas. It was in order to answer the need for a craft that could operate in deeper waters that the MS *(Motosilurante)* boats were introduced in 1941, designed and built by the CRDA, Monfalcone, yard. These were patterned on the German *Schnellboot* and resulted from the capture by the Italian navy in April 1941 of six Yugoslavian boats that had been built in Germany between 1935-39. They were some ninety feet overall, powered by three Isotta Fraschini engines of 3,450 horse-power which gave a speed of thirty-four knots, armed with two or four 20mm/65 machine-guns, two 21-inch torpedoes (later craft carried an additional two 17.7-inch torpedoes), and from twelve to twenty depth charges. Plans had been drawn up for even larger MS-boats, but were cancelled after Italy's surrender in 1943. At that time, all the boats then in service were either transferred to the Germans, captured by them, or scuttled.

Another type of larger motor torpedo boat, also ninety feet long, was developed and built by Baglietto after Italy's entry into the war for the specific purpose of submarine hunting. Known as VAS *(Vedette Anti-Sommergibile)* boats, they were powered by two Fiat engines with an auxiliary Carraro engine which gave a speed of some nineteen knots, armed with two 20mm/65 machine-guns, four 8mm submachine-guns, two 17.7-inch torpedoes and thirty depth charges. Later types of this boat were powered by one Isotta Fraschini and two Carraro engines, which gave approximately the same speed. A number that were building in 1943 were captured by the Germans and later commissioned by the German navy as motor launches and minesweepers.

Germany had also become interested in the possibilities of motor torpedo boats in the late 1920s, partly because the Versailles Treaty limited not only the number but also the size of the warships that could be built for the German navy. In 1928, the *Reichsmarine* obtained from the Lürssen shipyard in Vegesack the plans of a luxury motor cruiser that was being built privately for an American customer, powered by three Maybach engines with a speed of over thirty knots. It was from this basic design that the *Schnellboot* was later developed. Germany had a great advantage over the other powers in possessing the Daimler-Benz diesel engine which could be adapted for use in small boats. Diesels were used to

power S-boats from the very beginning, and proved far less hazardous in operation than the highly inflammable petrol engined craft of other countries. At the same time, Lürssen concentrated on one basic type of craft, a combined motor torpedo boat and motor gunboat which could be used for a variety of purposes, while Britain and to a lesser extent America experimented with many different types of craft from different designers, with all the maintenance and supply problems that inevitably resulted from such a policy.

S1 was completed in 1930, a hard chine boat, eighty-one feet long, powered by three 1,000bhp diesel engines giving a top speed of thirty-seven knots, and armed with two

The first MGBs were converted from British Power Boat Company anti-submarine craft

21-inch torpedoes and a light machine-gun. Five more of these craft were built up to 1932 and formed into the 1st Flotilla under *Kapitänleutnant* Bey. But trials had revealed their inability to operate in heavy seas, so a larger craft was built, 106 feet in length, of round bilge design with two or three skins of teak on light metal frames and the engines increased to 1,320bhp. The wheelhouse became enclosed, a 20mm anti-aircraft gun took the place of the light machine-gun, and the crew was increased to twenty-one. Eight of these boats were built in 1934, then the size was again

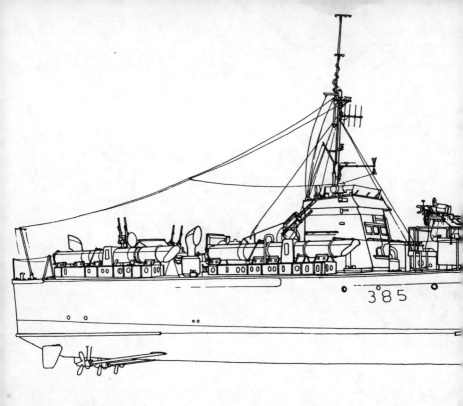

Vosper MTB: Second Series
Dimensions: 72½ feet by 19¼ feet. *Crew:* 12. *Engine:* Three Packard petrol motors, 3,600/4,050bhp. *Speed:* 38/40 knots. *Armament:* Two 21-inch torpedo tubes, one twin 0·5-inch gun, two twin 0.303-inch machine guns

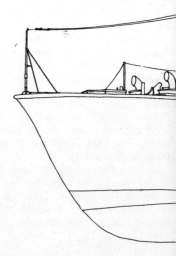

Vosper MTB: Third Series
Flush-decked. *Dimensions:* 73 feet by 19½ feet. *Crew:* 13. *Engine:* Three Packard petrol motors, 3,600/4,050bhp. *Speed:* 34/40 knots. *Armament:* Four 18-inch torpedo tubes, one manually operated, twin 20mm gun forward, two 0.5-inch guns, two twin 0.303-inch machine guns

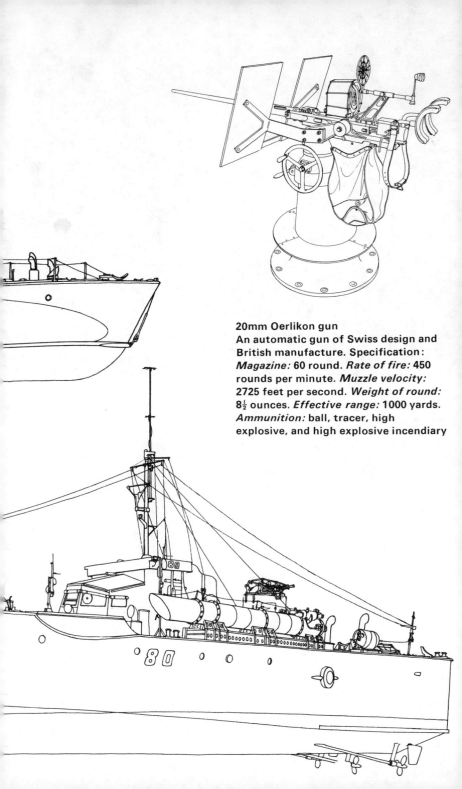

20mm Oerlikon gun
An automatic gun of Swiss design and
British manufacture. Specification:
Magazine: 60 round. *Rate of fire:* 450
rounds per minute. *Muzzle velocity:*
2725 feet per second. *Weight of round:*
$8\frac{1}{2}$ ounces. *Effective range:* 1000 yards.
Ammunition: ball, tracer, high
explosive, and high explosive incendiary

Above: Upper steering position of a Vosper MTB. *Right:* The lower steering position showing throttle controls

increased to 114 feet, partly to accommodate the more powerful diesel engines that had become available and which now gave a total of 6,150bhp and speeds of forty knots. Nineteen of these boats had been built by 1939.

These twenty-four craft (S1 had been scrapped) were the only motor torpedo boats in service with the German navy when the war began, and the first five were already obsolete. But a new series was already under construction at the Lürssen yard, similar in basic design but carrying four 21-inch torpedoes with the forward torpedo tubes enclosed by a partially raised forecastle. The first of these boats, S26, came into service early in 1940, and more than one hundred more were built over the next three years, mostly by Lürssen but a number also by the Schlichting yard at Travemünde, with only slight modifications. In 1943 a 40mm cannon

was added in place of one of the 20mm AA guns, the crew increased to twenty-three, and three new diesel engines which now gave a total of 7,500bhp resulted in an increase of speed to forty-two knots. Length was also slightly increased to 115 feet. Seventy-five of these craft were brought into service in 1943 and 1944. Later boats carried two 30mm AA guns in place of the former armament, and their speed was increased still further to forty-five knots with the introduction of 3,000bhp engines. A limited number of smaller craft of 92 feet and 108 feet were also built.

Armament was steadily increased as the war progressed and the S-boats found themselves under attack both from the air and from Allied MTBs and MGBs. Combinations of guns varied between one 40mm and three 20mm; and one 37mm and five 20mm; and finally three twin 30mm guns on the 1945 craft, which also carried four 21-inch torpedo tubes. Altogether, 244 S-boats were brought into service during the war.

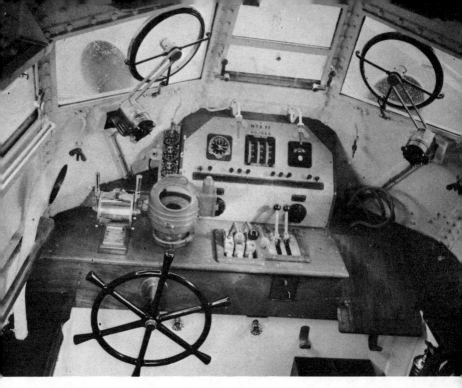

The German navy also developed another type of coastal craft, known as the R-boat (*Raumboot*). This was similar to the British ML, and was used for coastal convoy escort. mine-laying and minesweeping, and air-sea rescue. The first was built in 1934 by Lürssen. During the war, 325 R-boats were commissioned, of between 116 and 134 feet, powered by two or three-shaft diesels giving speeds of up to 24 knots, and armed variously with 37mm and 20mm AA guns.

In Britain meanwhile, the Royal Navy had in 1937 ordered twelve more of the British Power Boat Company's sixty-foot MTBs. Six were shipped to Hong Kong and formed into the 2nd MTB Flotilla. The others were intended for Singapore, but as they had only reached the Mediterranean by the summer of 1939, when war seemed inevitable, they were instead allocated to the 1st Flotilla at Malta to bring its number up to twelve.

With the Admiralty's increasing interest in small boats, other British yards were now competing for orders.

Two MTBs were built as private ventures. One was a sixty-eight foot craft by Commander du Cane's Vosper company. The other was by Scott-Paine's British Power Boat Company, a seventy-footer, larger than the eighteen boats they had originally supplied, and powered by Rolls Royce engines. The contract was eventually awarded to Vosper, whose design formed the basis for most of the 'short' MTBs used by the Royal Navy during the war, as distinct from the 'long' (over one hundred feet) MTBs built by other companies. Over 200 Vosper boats were eventually built and commissioned, including a few taken over by the Royal Navy at the beginning of the war that were being built for Norway and Greece. The Vosper yards could not by themselves cope with all the numbers required. Boats were also built to Vosper designs by other British boatyards, as well as in America. This was one of the advantages of small fighting craft, that they could be built quickly and in large numbers by relatively small

Left: A 6-pounder as mounted on the later Vosper MTBs. *Above:* Twin 20mm Oerlikons

boatyards round the coast, leaving the shipyards free to concentrate on building bigger warships.

Modifications in design were continually being made as new equipment and armament came into service. But there were three basic series of Vosper craft; seventy feet, seventy-two and a half feet, and finally seventy-three feet.

The seventy-footers were developed from the experimental boat built in 1937 which was chosen by the Admiralty after extensive trials the following year. They were powered by three Isotta Fraschini petrol engines totalling 3,600bhp giving a top speed of over forty knots, armed with two twin .5-inch guns and two 21-inch torpedoes and carrying a crew of ten. The first were built in 1939 and began to come into service the following year.

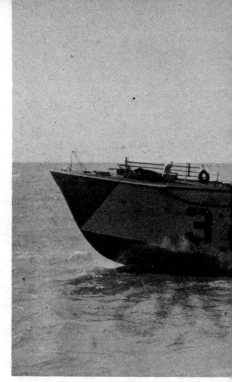

The greatest difficulty had been with the engines, and this was to remain a problem throughout the war. There were no suitable diesel engines available and so petrol engines had to be used, exposing the craft to the risk of fire and explosion when hit. But even with petrol engines, there were no suitable British power units available in the quantities required. Vosper's used the Isotta Fraschini engine to begin with, but supplies of these naturally ceased when Italy entered the war. Super-charged Hall Scott engines were used for a time until Packard engines could be obtained from America, the first of them arriving in 1941. Thereafter, these were used to power virtually all the British MTBs and MGBs, both short and long boats, as they also powered the American PT boats.

The second series of seventy-two

The three main types of Vosper MTB's
Above: The first were 70 feet armed with two 21-inch torpedo tubes, a twin .5-inch and two single .303-inch machine guns. *Right:* The second series were 72½ feet, carried twin 20mm guns and were powered by three 1,200hp Packard engines

and a half-foot boats began to come into service in 1942. The three Packard engines of 4,050bhp gave a top speed of forty knots. They were armed with one twin .5-inch and two twin .303 machine guns (the machine-guns were later exchanged for one 20mm and then a 6-pounder was also added), and carried two 21-inch torpedoes, with a crew of twelve which was later brought up to thirteen. These boats were also fitted with two Ford V8 engines by which means they could be driven silently at about six knots in order to make a quiet approach to the enemy without being detected. But in 1943, the main

The third series were 73 feet, flush-decked, and carried four 18-inch torpedo tubes

engines of the boats in service were fitted with silencers, which did away with the need for the auxiliary engines.

The seventy-three-footers came into service in 1944. They were powered by Packard engines which gave similar speeds, but the armament was increased to one twin 20mm, one twin .5-inch, two twin .303 machine-guns, and four 18-inch torpedoes. They carried a crew of thirteen.

In addition to the Vosper boats, short MTBs were also built by Thornycroft and J S White, some of which were building for other navies but taken over by the Royal Navy on the outbreak of war. A number of Elco and Higgins boats were also obtained under lend-lease from the United States.

Within the type known as short boats was the motor gunboat, equipped with heavier guns in place of torpedoes for the purpose of combating the German motor torpedo boats which threatened British coastal convoys. They were developed from the motor anti-submarine boats (MA/SBs) which had begun to be built in 1938 and 1939 by the British Power Boat Company when it seemed possible that enemy submarines might operate in the English Channel. These boats were a twin-screw version of the same company's sixty foot MTB, sacrificing speed and torpedoes in favour of anti-submarine weapons. It soon became apparent however that air patrols were sufficient to keep enemy submarines away from coastal waters. In 1940, the twenty-two MA/SBs then completed were converted into MGBs, armed with two twin .5-inch machine-guns and either one 2-pounder, one 20mm, or four .303 machine-guns.

But there was a demand for a fast MGB designed as such, rather than craft converted from other purposes. The British Power Boat Company set about drawing up plans, and in 1942 the first specifically designed MGBs came into service. They were seventy-one and a half feet overall, powered by three Packard engines of 4,050bhp which gave a top speed of forty knots, and armed with one 2-pounder, one twin 20mm, and two twin .303 machine-guns, and carried two depth charges. Over seventy were built during that year.

Fairmile B motor launch on anti-submarine patrol

**Six hundred of these Harbour Defence
motor launches were built and used
by British and Commonwealth navies
in many parts of the world**

M.L.1234

The long MTBs and MGBs, as boats of over one hundred feet were designated, were a development of the Fairmile 'A' motor launch, a 110-foot craft designed by Norman Hart which came to be used for many varied purposes, including convoy escort and minelaying. A Fairmile 'C' type came into service as the first long MGB in 1941. But it was the Fairmile 'D' – the 'dog-boat' as it was called – which became the most widely used of the bigger boats. Over 220 were built between 1942-1944. They were of prefabricated construction, 115 feet overall, powered by four Packard supercharged engines. They were able to operate in much heavier seas than the short boats, but because of their size and heavier armament they paid a penalty in speed, which was no more than about thirty knots. The 'D' boats were used variously as MTBs and MGBs, but eventually combined these functions and as such became the most heavily armed boats of their kind in the world, carrying two 6-pounders, one twin 20mm, two twin .5-inch and two .303 machine-guns, and four 18-inch torpedoes.

An even larger craft, the Denny-type steam gunboat (SGB) which was 145 feet long, came into service in 1942. But these were not very successful, being too slow and too large for the kind of small boat fighting for which they were intended, and only seven were built.

In America, meanwhile, as a result of winning the 1938 competition to build PT boats, the Higgins company was going ahead on building two eighty–one–foot craft while other boats were being built experimentally by the US Navy. Then, in 1939, the British Power Boat Company sold to the US Navy its private venture seventy-foot MTB and it was arranged for this to be built under licence by Elco. Modifications were made, including the substitution of Packard engines for the original Rolls Royce engines and an increase in length to eighty feet. At the same time, Higgins

re-designed their craft, which now became seventy-eight feet and followed the hard chine stepless bottom hull and outward flare at the sides of the original Scott-Paine boat from the British Power Boat Company.

From 1941 onwards, these two boats, the Elco eighty-footer and the Higgins seventy-eight-footer, became standard types for the American fleet. Over 300 of the first and over 200 of the second type were eventually built. Both were powered by three twelve cylinder Packard marine engines, originally of 1,200hp each but later increased to 1,500hp in order to maintain the design speed of forty knots when heavier armament was installed. Although both followed a similar basic design each craft had its own distinctive below-deck arrangement. The Elco boat was slightly faster, but the Higgins was more manoeuvrable, so that depending on the conditions under which they were used each had its own proponents who thought the one better than the other. The first boats carried four torpedo tubes – 18-inch to begin with, then 21-inch – and two twin .5-inch machine-guns. An increase in gun-armament was made possible by a reduction in the weight of torpedo equipment when the Mark XIII torpedo was introduced in place of the original Mark VIII, a far more accurate weapon which could be launched from simple racks on either side of a boat instead of through the heavy and cumbersome torpedo tubes. Thus the later boats were equipped with a 20mm cannon, then automatic 37mm guns, and were still able to maintain their speeds. After 1943 these guns were replaced by two 40mm cannons, and towards the end of the war experiments were being made with 75mms, 4.5-inch barrage rocket projectors, and 5-inch spin-stabilised rockets.

The Japanese, hampered by the lack of suitable engines, did less than any of the major powers in developing motor torpedo boats. Most of the small craft built before the war were of the landing craft type, intended primarily for use during the invasion of China and later during the invasions of the Philippines and New Guinea.

As a result of capturing one of the Thornycroft CMBs at Canton in 1938, the Japanese did build an experimental motor torpedo boat which led to the T-1 type, fifty-nine feet in length, powered by two 1,800hp petrol engines which gave thirty-eight knots and armed with two machine-guns and two 18-inch torpedoes. Seven of these were built in 1941. Later craft, including the much bigger T-51 type which was 104 feet long, were simplified so that they could be constructed quickly by small boatyards. But without more powerful engines available, they were only capable of between seventeen and twenty-seven knots. Many hulls were completed for which no engines at all were available, so that they were still on the stocks at the end of the war.

As a result of acquiring a former Italian MAS boat in 1940, the Japanese also developed several types of motor gunboat, powered by aircraft engines which gave between seventeen and thirty-four knots. Most of these were about sixty feet long and armed with machine guns and carried two or four depth charges. But again the shortage of engines severely restricted the number that could be brought into service.

During the closing stages of the war, as a last resort, the Japanese introduced the *Shinyo* type one-man suicide boat. This was no more than a sixteen foot motor boat, powered by one or two automobile engines with speeds of up to thirty knots and loaded with TNT in the bows; it was intended to be driven on a collision course with an enemy vessel. Over 6,000 were built, most of them in 1944 for use during the Okinawa campaign. But the American PT boats usually managed to locate and destroy them in their hiding-places before they could even be used, and there is no record of any Allied ship being seriously damaged by them.

These boats, the British MTBs and MGBs, the American PTs, the German S-boats and Italian MAS-boats, were the main types of small fighting craft used in the Second World War. From small beginnings they were built up into formidable fleets that fought some of the fiercest sea battles of the war. And the first areas in which they saw active service were the coastal waters of the North Sea and the English Channel.

Controls of a Vosper 73-foot MTB

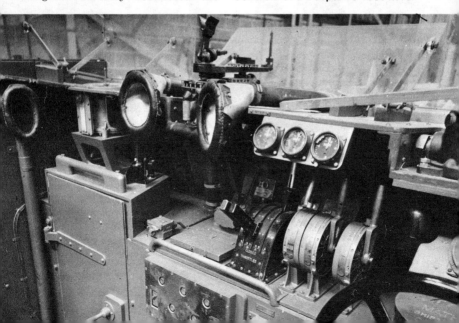

Above and below: Packard engines powered most of the British and American boats *Right:* A schooner re-arms an MTB

Torpedo tubes under construction

Fight for the narrow seas

The war in Europe began with the opposing motor torpedo boat forces much the same in number – the British had twenty-two boats in service, the Germans twenty-four. All were some distance from what was to become their main area of operations. The only fully operational British flotilla was at Malta, while the German boats were based at Wilhelmshaven, confined during the winter of 1939-40 to carrying out uneventful patrols off the north coast of Germany.

The 1st MTB Flotilla was recalled from the Mediterranean in November 1939. After a spectacular voyage by way of the Rhône, the French canals to Paris, and down the Seine to the Channel, they arrived at Portsmouth on 8th December. One boat had been lost en route during a gale off Sardinia – the first MTB casualty of the war.

At Portsmouth, the new seventy-foot Vosper boats were being formed into the 4th Flotilla. The older sixty-foot boats of the 1st Flotilla were refitted and made their way to Felixstowe on the east coast of England, which in January 1940 became the first operational MTB base. But there was very little opportunity for action. The enemy submarines which had been expected to operate in coastal waters were in the main kept away by air patrols, and in any case the Germans intended to concentrate their U-boats on attacking Atlantic convoys. So the MTBs were used for a variety of tasks, such as air-sea rescue and ferrying messages and supplies amongst the ships of the Home Fleet.

There was at this time a desperate shortage of vessels suitable for escorting Britain's vast fleet of merchant ships. Every day convoys of about forty ships, strung out over ten miles, would set out along the east coast routes, escorted by no more than a couple of destroyers and, when they became available, a few MLs.

The Germans on the other hand faced a different situation. They had many more escort vessels than merchant ships, including destroyers, torpedo boats, armed trawlers, as well as the S-and R-boats. A German convoy of two or three merchant ships was usually protected by six or more escorts. This was to set the pattern for the fight for the narrow seas over the next three years. The Germans not only had a greater number of targets on the British side which they could attack, but they could use their S-boats more aggressively for this purpose without depleting the forces available to protect their own convoys.

And so it was that on the night of 9th May, when for the first time a patrol of four S-boats made the long journey south from Wilhelmshaven into the English Channel, they struck the first blow with a torpedo attack on a British destroyer, *Kelly*. The German boats were led by *Kapitän-leutnant* Rudolph Petersen, who was later to become one of the best known S-boat aces and eventually took over command of all the S-boat flotillas.

The *Kelly* was very badly damaged and it was only by the skill of her crew that she did not sink and was brought back to port after a tow lasting ninety-one hours. This example of what a small torpedo boat could do against even a destroyer came as a shock to the British Admiralty. And when, the next day, the Germans invaded Holland and Belgium and it seemed only a matter of time before France fell, it was realised that the S-boats would be right on Britain's doorstep. They would no longer have to make the 400-mile round trip from Wilhelmshaven. They would have bases all along the coast of Western Europe from which it was only a short haul to attack British coastal shipping.

It was at this point that, for the first time, serious consideration was given to the threat from German S-boats. The MA/SB craft previously intended for submarine hunting were rapidly converted into motor gunboats to combat the S-boats. Orders were also given for the construction of boats specifically designed as MGBs. But it would be another eighteen months before these came into service. In the meantime, the task would have to be shouldered by a few MTBs and ex-MA/SBs, most of which were armed with nothing heavier than .303 machine-guns against the 20mm guns of the German boats.

The evacuation from Dunkirk at the end of May gave the little ships their first opportunity for action. Every available boat in Britain was called upon to take part in the evacuation and these included seven MTBs, three MA/SBs, one ML, and one old CMB. Their main task was to patrol the eastern flank of the beachhead to hold off the marauding S-boats. Some of the commanders present were men whose names were to become legendary in the war of the little ships, like Stewart Gould, Christopher Dreyer, Bill Everitt, Hillary Gamble, and Harpy Lloyd. One of them, John Cameron, was the last to leave Dunkirk, in a forty-foot MTB that was one of the smallest craft to take part in the operation.

But their forces were too few and too ill-equipped to keep the S-boats permanently at bay. Amongst other ships, they sunk two British destroyers, *Wakeful* and *Grafton*. One of the boats, S25, was commanded by Siegfried Wuppermann, another German ace who was to become well known for his exploits in the Mediterranean.

After Dunkirk, German S-boat bases were rapidly established at Boulogne, Cherbourg, Le Havre, Ijmuiden, Ostend and Rotterdam. In Britain meanwhile, further MTB bases were also being established, at Harwich, Dover, Fort William, Portland and Fowey. The little ships faced each other across the waters of the English Channel, the Dover Straits, and the North Sea, in some places no more than thirty miles apart. The fight for the narrow seas was about to begin in earnest.

At this time, there existed no established techniques for motor torpedo boat fighting in either the British or German navies. The commanders and their crews, who were for the most part volunteers and recruits, had to learn by trial and error. Although increasing numbers of boats were coming into service as the British and German war-building programmes got under way, there were no organisations to co-ordinate the training of crews and the manning of craft. In Britain, the flotillas came under the authority of individual Commanders-in-Chief who used them as they thought best, and only in November 1940 was Coastal Forces formed, with Rear-Admiral Piers Kekewich in command, to bring some degree of control over their operations. In Germany, the S-boat flotillas came under the overall control of the Commander of Torpedo-boats, *Konteadmiral* Bütow, and it was not until April 1942 that a separate *Schnellboote* command was established,

HMS *Kelly* on tow after being torpedoed by a German S-boat

Men of Coastal Forces. *Above left:* Lieutenant-Commander R P Hichens. *Above right:* Lieutenant P F S Gould. *Below left:* Lieutenant-Commander E N Pumphrey *Below right:* Lieutenant E D W Leaf

Above left: Lieutenant-Commander P M Scott. *Above right:* Lieutenant D G H Wright. *Below left:* Able Seaman Lamont, veteran rating aged 60. *Below right:* Lieutenant G J MacDonald

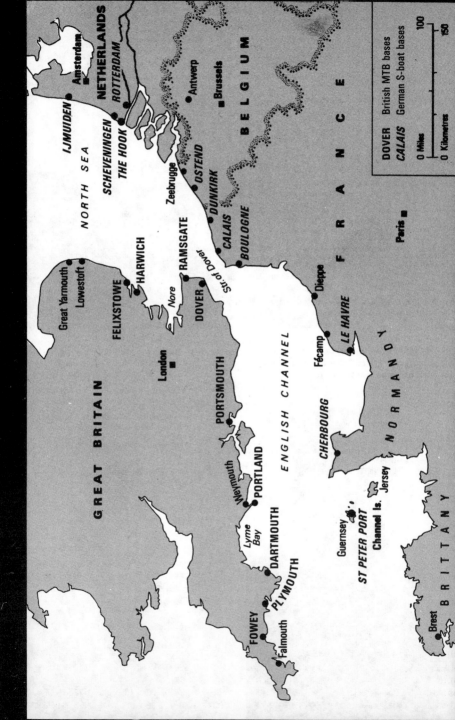

with *Kommodore* Rudolph Petersen as Commander-in-Chief.

The MTB patrols carried out early in the year were mainly uneventful but on 8th September 1940, the MTBs made their first successful torpedo attack. This was against a large German convoy anchored off Ostend, and was achieved by two boats from Felixstowe, MTB 15 (Lieutenant J A Cardley-Wilmot RNVR) and MTB 17 (Lieutenant R I T Faulkner RNVR). Because the RAF were also carrying out a bombing raid on the vessels at the same time, it was difficult to assess exactly the number of ships hit by torpedoes, but the MTBs certainly sank at least one ammunition ship and one supply ship.

Further attacks during the following three months on German vessels anchored off Dutch harbours resulted in the sinking of two armed trawlers, a large supply ship and a flak ship, and damage to another supply ship. After that, the Germans became more careful about leaving merchant ships anchored in exposed positions, and nearly a year passed before the next MTB action, in September 1941.

The Germans meanwhile had not been slow in exploiting their earlier success. Although it was not until the late summer of 1941 that they began to attack the British east coast convoys in earnest, during 1940 they sank no less than twenty-three British merchant ships. And even more dangerous were the mines which they frequently laid off the east and south coasts, responsible for sinking at least another 40,000 tons of shipping.

The operations by both the British and German boats during this time revealed only too clearly the lack of training and understanding in the kind of tactics required. Torpedoes would be fired at too great a distance from their targets to have much chance of scoring a hit. Craft sometimes collided at sea. And since they operated mostly at night to avoid air patrol and identification was not always easy, it sometimes happened that boats of the same side fired on each other.

But the crews were learning from such mistakes. They found for instance that while approaching a target from behind might have an advantage in that the enemy usually kept a poorer lookout in that direction, the ideal firing position was from an angle in front of the enemy's bow. With the whole length of the target exposed, there was the maximum margin for error and the enemy had the greatest distance to turn in order to take avoiding action. The actual firing angle had of course to take account of a number of factors, including the speeds of the torpedo and the target and the distance the torpedo had to travel. It meant that the torpedo had to be aimed some distance ahead of the target.

Getting into this ideal firing position was another matter, of course. If a motor torpedo boat came up at full speed, she would be detected from some distance off, either from the noise of her engines or the foaming wake that such a speed created. The enemy merchant ships would turn away while the escorts intervened and engaged the MTBs in a gun-fight for which they were ill-equipped.

It was found that a far more successful approach was to creep up slowly and quietly on auxiliary engines, preferably from the dark horizon so so that the moon, if there was one, would light the enemy's path. In this way a boat could often get to within a few hundred yards of the enemy without being seen. The torpedoes would be fired, then the main engines crash-started to enable the boat to disengage at top speed, possibly laying a smoke-screen as additional cover.

The silent approach came to be the most effective technique in MTB operations. As there was always a dangerous moment as the auxiliary engines were de-clutched and the main engines started, later types of craft had silencers fitted to the main engines themselves. In this way a

silent approach could be made by idling in on just the centre engine. When speed was required, this could be accelerated and the wing engines started in much less time than it had taken to change over from auxiliaries.

Another favoured technique was to divide the attacking force into two separate units. One would approach at full speed from the opposite direction without any attempt at concealment and thus draw the enemy's fire, while the second unit crept in quietly to make the actual torpedo attack. If the second unit was sighted, then the positions would be reversed according to a pre-arranged plan; the second unit would increase speed and engage the enemy with guns in order to create as much confusion as possible while the first would revert to a silent approach.

Yet another method was to wait with engines cut in the expected path of a convoy until the enemy ships came up and presented suitable targets. The danger here was that the waiting boats might find themselves

Opposing forces: British and German MTBs head out on patrol into the North Sea

stationary targets in the middle of a group of escorts, unable to start their engines and get away in time before being attacked. And it also meant that they had to have a good idea of the location of the approaching convoy. It was not easy to make contact with the enemy, especially on nights when visibility was poor. Patrols would go out night after night for months on end in a fruitless search for enemy targets. Boats could pass unseen within a few hundred yards of one another at night.

In this respect however, Britain possessed a great advantage as radar came to be developed. The southern commands in particular came to build up a highly efficient system of RDF (radio direction finding) in the English Channel, so that enemy convoys could be located as they tried to make the run through the Dover Strait. It was n this way that MTBs of the 6th flotilla based at Dover achieved the first major success for Coastal Forces n the night of 8th September 1941.

Earlier that evening, Dover Command had received RDF reports of German convoy leaving Boulogne and heading northwards through the over Staits. Only three MTBs were operational at the time, MTB 35, commanded by Lieutenant-Commander Edward N Pumphrey RN, Senior Officer of the flotilla, MTB 218 (Lieutenant C E 'Chuck' Bonnell, Royal Canadian Naval Volunteer Reserve), and MTB 54 (Lieutenant Per Danielsen, Royal Norwegian Navy). They set out from Dover and shortly after 23.30, guided by RDF reports from base, they were lying in wait with engines cut in the path of the approaching convoy.

As the enemy ships loomed out of the darkness, they were seen to be two large merchant vessels escorted by two armed trawlers and at least eight S-boats. In the first torpedo attack one of the merchant vessels was sunk, almost before the enemy had become aware of the presence of the MTBs. The MTBs disengaged, then later, joined by two MGBs from Ramsgate under the command of Lieutenant Stewart Gould RN, which fought a gun battle with the S-boats, they made another attack and sunk the second merchant vessel and one of the armed trawlers. The British craft sustained only slight damage.

This operation set a pattern for future MTB operations in the Channel. Attacks were not always so successful, but they made the Germans very wary about ship movements in the Channel and those convoys that did make the run had to be heavily escorted.

In the North Sea however, it was the S-boats which had the upper hand. They were employed for most of the

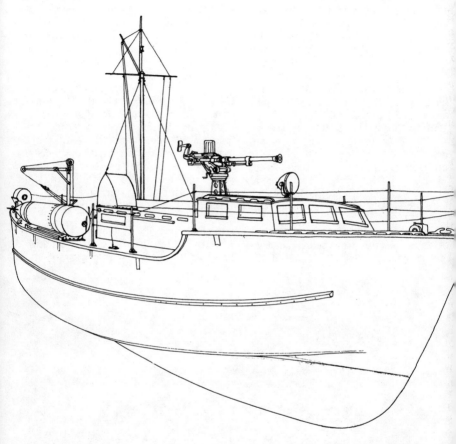

Japanese MTB
Based on the design of a captured First World War Thornycroft CMB.
Armament: Two 18.7-inch torpedo tubes, one 20mm automatic cannon model 98
(1938), and light machine guns

me laying mines off the east coast of ngland. But they also made torpedo ttacks on British convoys when the ccasion presented itself and sank ver a dozen ships in this way during 41. There was little to stand in their ay except for a few flotillas of the onverted MA/SBs, not really suited the task. These boats might have een used as convoy escorts, but there as a very real danger that they ight be mistaken for S-boats and red at by their own forces. They were nt out to patrol a line some six iles off the convoy routes in the hope f intercepting the S-boats. But with eir faster speed, the S-boats usually anaged to slip through. The MGBs ere seldom able to make contact, nd when they did the S-boats, whose ommanders had orders to avoid action ith the British craft, invariably anaged to get away.

And then, on the night of 19th/20th ovember, after months of frustra- on, the MGBs scored their first ecisive victory over the S-boats and ok a step towards regaining control coastal waters in the North Sea. his action also brought to public otice the name of a man who was to ecome the best known of all those ho served in Coastal Forces – Lieu- nant-Commander Robert P Hichens NVR.

Hichens had already won his first SC for his work on the beaches uring the Dunkirk evacuation, at hich time he was serving in a mine- weeper. Now he was commander of e 6th MGB Flotilla based at Felix- owe. On this particular night, he was harbour when reports came through at S-boats had been seen in the cinity of the east coast convoy utes. He set out immediately in his wn boat, MGB 64, with MGB 67 ieutenant L G R Campbell RNVR) d MGB 63 (Lieutenant G E Bailey NVP).

The object was to engage the enemy quickly as possible. But first ailey's boat broke down with engine ouble and had to turn back, then one

of the engines in Hichens' own boat broke down and his maximum speed was reduced to eighteen knots. There was no chance of reaching the enemy in time, so instead Hichens led the two boats to a point where he thought the S-boats might pass when returning to their Dutch base.

It was not until 4.45 on the morning of the 20th, after lying in wait with engines cut for more than two hours, that the sound of the returning S-boats was heard. Five of them ap-peared, moving slowly, as they had arrived at their rendezvous position after their night's work. It was this that gave the MGBs their chance. In the normal way, the forty knots of the S-boats was too great a speed for the British craft, and in any case Hichens' boat was reduced to less than half speed because of engine failure.

The two MGBs surged in amongst the S-boats before the Germans were aware of what was happening. They were two against five, by far out-gunned and out-classed by the bigger German craft. But they did have the advantage of surprise and the sheer determination of Hichens to make the most of this opportunity after a year's search for the elusive enemy.

The S-boats were raked by gunfire at a range of fifty yards. Their return fire was erratic and passed harmlessly over the MGBs. Then they somewhat recovered and scattered in all direc-tions, having sustained considerable damage. Just how much was apparent an hour or so later when, after head-ing for the Dutch coast in the hope of making contact again, the MGBs came across one S-boat which had been left abandoned. She had been so badly damaged that she was sinking, her crew having been taken off by other boats. Hichens tried to keep her afloat so that she could be towed back to England, but she was already too far down in the water. Reluctantly they had to stand off and watch her sink.

This encounter, which proved that the S-boats could be taken on and beaten in a straight fight put new

heart into Coastal Forces. The MGBs began increasingly to make contact with the enemy, particularly when the faster and better armed gunboats came into service in 1942. Hichens went on to serve with great distinction, not only as a flotilla leader but as the originator of much of the tactical theory on which motor gunboat warfare developed. He was awarded the DSO twice and the DSC three times, and was three times mentioned in dispatches.

He was offered senior posts ashore, but preferred to remain in action with the boats he loved so much, and of which he wrote:

'I think one of the most lovely sights I have ever seen is a gunboat unit at speed in the moonlight, with the white pluming wakes, the cascading bow waves, the thick black outlines of the guns darkly silhouetted, the figures of the gunners motionless at their positions as though carved out of black rock, all against the beautiful setting of the moon-path on the water.'

Hichens was killed in the early hours of 13th April 1943 by a final burst of enemy fire after a minor engagement had been broken off. He had taken part in 148 operations, of which fourteen were actions against the enemy.

The summer and autumn of 1942 saw the fight between the little ships reach its peak in the North Sea and English Channel, with battles raging almost nightly. The year had begun with the S-boats in the ascendancy. Then the balance evened up, and towards the end of the year it began to swing in favour of the British.

By this time there were fourteen MTB and thirteen MGB flotillas of eight boats each operating from twenty Coastal Force bases along the eastern and southern coasts of Britain, and the first of the long boats, the 'D' type Fairmiles, were coming into service. Ranged against these forces were similar numbers of S-boats and R-boats, which for much of the time concentrated on laying mines in the British shipping routes. During the first six months of the year they laid 260 magnetic and acoustic mines off the east coast alone, responsible for the sinking of more than thirty Allied merchant ships as well as the escort destroyer *Vimiera*. They sank further ships by direct torpedo attack, including another destroyer the *Vortigern*.

Meanwhile, the MTBs in the English Channel, often operating in combination with the MGBs, were keeping up their own attacks on German convoys. It became a hazardous undertaking for the enemy to try to slip through the Dover Straits. When on 12th May a German armed merchant raider was escorted through by four torpedo boats, eight minesweepers, and many smaller craft, two of the torpedo boats, *Iltis* and *Seadler* were sunk for the loss of one MTB. Later in the year, the armed merchant raider *Komet* was sunk by MTB 236 (Sub-Lieutenant R Q Drayson RNVR) while attempting to make the same passage.

These successes made up in part for the failure in January to stop the battle-cruisers *Scharnhorst* and *Gneisenau* and the heavy cruiser *Prinz Eugen* from making the passage after breaking out from Brest. The MTBs had done their best, but they were kept at bay by a very large escort of destroyers, torpedo boats, and S-boats.

Because of the formidable opposition which the S-boats now regularly encountered from the patrolling MGBs, the Germans followed a policy of suddenly switching their main attacks from one area to another. In June, an S-boat flotilla began operating from Cherbourg in the Western Channel. This took the British by surprise, and when on 7th July the S-boats attacked a convoy in Lyme Bay, they torpedoed and sank six ships with no loss to themselves.

At this point, Hichens was transferred temporarily to the West Country with a new 8th MGB Flotilla operating

MGB on night patrol

Admiralty House,

Portsmouth.

No.7910/87.

15th June, 1940.

Dear Sirs,

I enclose an extract of a report
from the Commanding Officer, H.M.S. HORNET and
have much pleasure in endorsing his opinion with
regard to M.T.B. 102 in particular, and Vosper's
M.T.B.'s generally.

I should be glad if you could convey
the Commanding Officer, H.M.S. HORNET's remarks
to all concerned.

Yours faithfully

Admiral.

Messrs. Vospers Ltd.,
Portsmouth.

EXTRACT FROM H.M.S. HORNET'S REPORT.

x.x x x x x x x x x x x x x x x x x x x

It may be of interest to the designers and builders of M.T.B. No.102 to know that she took an important part in the evacuation of the B.E.F. from Dunkirk. By Builders, I mean all the Vosper craftsmen and workmen who helped to build her, and are building British M.T.B's.

The fact that this boat, over three years old, attacked by German aircraft, by bombs and machine guns, going alongside piers already damaged by shellfire and bombs, and constantly being bombed and shelled, came out at the end of it unscathed, with hull and engines in perfect condition, is a tremendous tribute to the Firm and the workmanship.   M.T.B. 102 had many bombs dropped close to her, several within 10 yards, and one within two yards of her transom, and in spite of this, no defect developed.

Knowing this, one can imagine that con- fidence the M.T.B. Officers and Men have in Vosper M.T.B's.

x x x x x x x x x x x x x

Above: A 21-inch 'tin fish'. *Below:* An early German S-boat. Later types had their torpedo tubes built into the hull. *Right:* MGB s were also used for air/sea rescue

rom Dartmouth. In August after
everal successful encounters with
nemy merchant vessels, he scored a
decisive victory over the S-boats by
inking two of them and damaging
others in a twelve-minute action off
Cherbourg. Soon after this the
Germans transferred their main
activities back to the North Sea, and
Hichens returned to Felixstowe with
his flotilla in September.

His operations in the Western
Channel had shown this to be a fruit-
ful hunting ground for the MTBs. As
there was less danger from mines in
these deeper waters, destroyers could
operate in combination with the small
boats as had originally been envisaged. Strong forces of MTBs,
MGBs, and Hunt-class destroyers were
formed at Dartmouth, Plymouth and
Portsmouth. They carried out many
successful sorties amongst the Channel
Islands and between Cherbourg and
Ushant until eventually, after the
Normandy landings in 1944, the Channel
was cleared of enemy ships.

On resuming their main operations
in the North Sea, the S-boats found
the situation had greatly changed.
Coastal Forces not only had faster and
more heavily armed boats available,
but by the end of the year the whole
coastal area of Nore Command was
covered by radar. Enemy boats could
be detected and plotted up to twenty
miles offshore, so that the MGBs
could be sent out to intercept them
before they could reach the east coast
convoy routes. It was now rare for the
S-boats to slip through the patrol
lines.

At the same time, the MTBs were
becoming more successful in carrying
the attack against German convoys
off the coast of Western Europe. Some
of the most successful tactics in MTB
warfare were devised by the commander of the 21st MTB Flotilla at
Felixstowe, Lieutenant-Commander
Peter Dickens DSO, MBE, DSC, RN.
He approached the problem as that of
a hunter stalking a quarry, in which
the best method was not a blind, head-

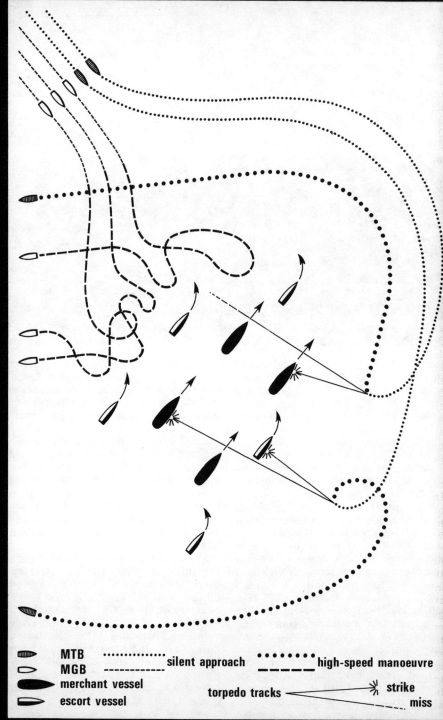

MTB
MGB
merchant vessel
escort vessel

silent approach
high-speed manoeuvre

torpedo tracks
strike
miss

ong rush forwards but a deliberate and unhurried approach. His first big success against an enemy convoy came on the night of 10th September. While three MGBs commanded by Lieutenant E D W Leaf DSC, RNVR engaged the escort vessels on one side, according to a pre-arranged plan, Dickens led two MTBs quietly in from the other side and sank a merchant ship and flak trawler without sustaining any hits themselves.

With the introduction of the larger 'D' type MTBs, capable of longer range and the ability to withstand heavier seas, a new area of operations was opened up against enemy shipping in the fjords on the Norwegian coast. The MTBs operated from the Shetlands, and the first flotilla to be formed there, the 30th, was manned by officers and men of the Royal Norwegian Navy under Lieutenant-Commander R A Tamber. This was later reinforced by a British flotilla, under Lieutenant-Commander K Gemmel RNVR. The first success came on 27th November 1942, when two large enemy merchant ships were sunk in the Skjaergaard fjord. Operations from the Shetlands continued until the last days of the war, and included not only torpedo attacks but participation in Commando raids on enemy coastal installations.

The employment of Coastal Forces craft in Commando raids was not new. In fact, this had been the kind of operation in which the little ships had proved themselves in the First World War, by the raids on Ostend and Zeebrugge. Similar in character to these were the two great Commando raids of 1942, that on St Nazaire in March and on Dieppe in August.

The St Nazaire raid on the night of 27th March was a masterpiece of combined operations planning. Its main purpose was to destroy the huge graving-dock which originally had been constructed in 1935 for the building of the French liner *Normandie* and was now the only dock outside Germany capable of accommodating the new German battleship *Tirpitz*. The presence of such a warship in these waters would have posed a grave threat to the Atlantic convoys.

Bombing raids by the RAF on the harbour at Brest had already forced the German cruisers *Scharnhorst*, *Gneisenau*, and *Prinz Eugen* to move into safer waters off the Norwegian coast – hence their dash through the Channel two months earlier. But the dock at St Nazaire was too solidly constructed and too heavily defended to be put out of action by bombing alone. Some other kind of attack was called for. And this eventually took the form of a Commando raid in which an obsolete destroyer, *Campbeltown*, was to be used to ram the enormous caisson at the entrance to the dock and destroy them by explosive charges loaded in the destroyer and timed to go off after the raiding party had departed.

Sixteen MLs, one MTB, and one MGB took part in the operation, escorted during the voyage across from Falmouth by two destroyers. Surprise was essential. In order to

An ideal mixed night operation – MTBs and MGBs engage a convoy. Having sighted the enemy the MTBs detach and move quietly to the far side of the convoy. After an interval to allow the MTBs to get well on their way, the MGBs – whose value as attackers of large vessels is negligible – execute a high speed feint attack with all guns and maximum noise, to draw the enemy's fire and decoy the escorts from the merchant ships. If still undetected the MTBs are now in position to deliver their torpedoes at close range, undistracted by the need to manoeuvre to avoid counter-attack. Once the torpedoes have struck, the main engines are crash started for immediate withdrawal

In the case of an attack by a group of MTBs alone the group splits up as described but each section approaches silently and the first to be spotted makes the feint attack, firing its torpedoes however if opportunity offers

create confusion just before the attack and to drown the noise of the approaching boats, it was planned for the RAF to carry out a diversionary bombing raid on the harbour. Unfortunately, when the planes arrived, the area was completely obscured by low cloud. The air crews were under express orders at that time not to make indiscriminate bombing attacks in occupied France unless targets could be clearly identified. They had no alternative but to return home with scarcely a bomb dropped.

This not only meant that the positive objectives of the air raid were unfulfilled, but far worse the attempt had raised the alarm and put the German defences on their guard.

They were thus prepared to meet the naval force when it arrived, and the intended element of surprise was lost.

Several hours of bitter fighting followed, in which nearly two-thirds of the attacking force of 630 naval and military personnel were either killed or taken prisoner. Only three MLs

survived to make the voyage home. Nearly all the men who were brought back were wounded. But although no all the objectives were achieved, such as the destruction of the submarine pens in the harbour, the main purpose of the raid succeeded brilliantly when the following morning the destroyer *Campbeltown* which had rammed the dock gates as planned, blew up with an enormous explosion, putting the dock out of commission for the rest of the war.

The year 1942 which had begun so disastrously for the Allies ended with Coastal Forces gaining at least a measure of mastery over the narrow seas separating Britain from Europe. A means had been found of combating the S-boat menace, and the MTBs were increasingly on the offensive against German coastal convoys. But by now, the little ships were fighting in other theatres as well. And in the Pacific, the American PT boats were also in action for the first time.

Controls of a German S-boat

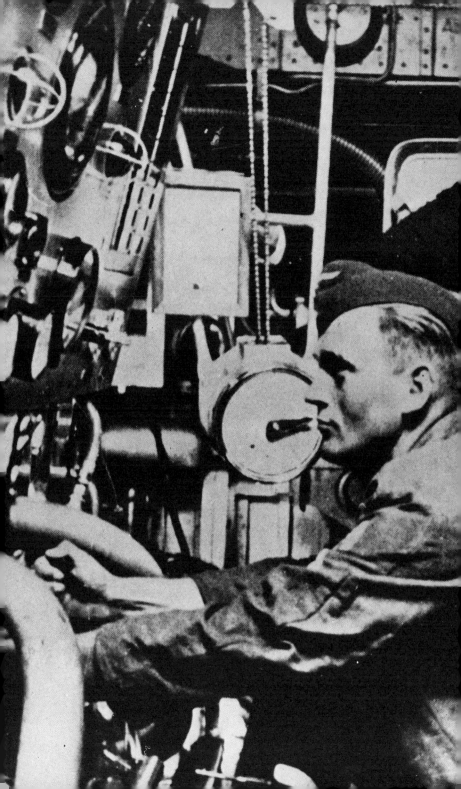

Hich's flotilla of MGBs

orpedo firing mechanisms under test

Above: The German S-boat captured by Lieutenant-Commander Hichens, which later sank. *Below:* Third series Vosper MTB

Above: Heavily armed Fairmile D combined MTB/MGB. **Below:** Torpedoes start their run

Above: Lieutenant Peter Dickens (centre) with his crew after leading a successful MTB attack on armed enemy trawlers off the Dutch coast
Below: Motor launch with crew at action stations: *Right:* Battle-scarred MTB

German *Räumboote* flotilla, minelaying off Norway

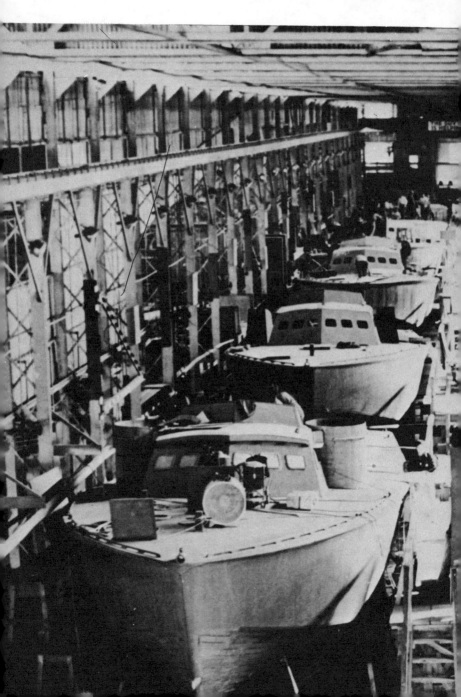

Japanese attack

When the Japanese suddenly struck on the morning of 7th December 1941 with attacks on Pearl Harbor, Hong Kong, the Philippines, and the invasions of Siam and Malaya, amongst the few naval craft which were in a position to fight back were American and British motor torpedo boats.

Based in Hong Kong were the six British Power Boat Company sixty-foot MTBs which had been formed into the 2nd MTB Flotilla after their arrival in 1938, together with two First World War CMBs acquired from the Chinese Navy. When war broke out in Europe, most of the other naval craft in Hong Kong had been transferred to Aden. The eight MTBs, graphically described by the local Chinese as 'wind thunder boats', were virtually the only naval defence left when the Japanese attacked.

Their first task was to help evacuate troops retreating along the Kowloon Peninsula, which was carried out at night to avoid the Japanese air patrols. But it was Japanese air supremacy that was responsible for the flotilla's first casualties, when during a bombing raid on their base at Aberdeen harbour on 15th December, one MTB and the headquarters ship *Cornflower* were sunk and two MTBs damaged.

Working in pairs, the MTBs maintained their patrols against overwhelming odds, frequently engaging enemy minesweepers which were clearing the Bay in preparation for an amphibious landing. This began on the morning of 19th December, and two MTBs, led by Lieutenant R R W Ashby HKRNVR, were sent to attack the craft ferrying Japanese troops across. Expecting little resistance, the Japanese were taken by surprise. In spite of heavy fire from the shore and from Japanese ships in Hong Kong harbour, the MTBs came speeding in amongst the invasion craft, shooting at anything that came into their sights and overturning many of the smaller boats in their wash.

Although damaged, the MTBs managed to return to base. Further attacks were made by other craft during the next five days. But the Japanese were now on the alert. The MTBs were invariably beaten off, and two of them blown up by direct hits. The end was inevitable. On 25th December, the day that Hong Kong fell, the five remaining boats of the flotilla left Aberdeen harbour. Without sufficient range to reach friendly territory, they were to be scuttled after their crews had been landed on the Chinese mainland. With them were a few survivors from a motor launch that had been sunk by the Japanese while trying to escape from Hong Kong, amongst whom was Admiral Sir Andrew Chen Chak, President of Southern Kuomintang. He was an elderly man with only one leg, but when the launch was attacked he had thrown his wooden leg over the side, jumped into the water after it, and managed to swim to shore.

By luck, the naval party landed on a part of the coast controlled by Chinese guerilla forces. Their only way of escape was across China to Rangoon - a journey of 3,000 miles. It would have been an impossible undertaking but for two unforeseen events – meeting up with the Chinese guerillas who could guide the party through Japanese occupied territory, and the presence of Chen Chak who could communicate with the guerillas and also help later when the party reached Free China.

The memorable journey took three months, and included travel on foot, by river junk, lorry and train. The party eventually reached Rangoon on 14th February – only to find that their arrival coincided with that of the Japanese. Singapore surrendered the following day, and Rangoon itself fell three weeks later. Most of the party were able to get away to serve with the navy in other theatres. Lieutenant Ashby joined Coastal Forces and saw service in the North Sea, the Mediterranean, and finally commanded Coastal Force operations along the Burma coast during the last Arakan campaign, by which time he had been promoted to Commander and awarded the DSC.

There were no MTBs stationed at Singapore and Rangoon. Those originally intended for Singapore had been re-assigned to Malta in 1939 and because of the urgent demand for coastal craft in home waters, they had not been replaced. The brunt of the Japanese attacks early in 1942 were borne by a few outdated MLs, manned by the Dominion and Colonial RNVR. They fought for as long as they could against the greatly superior enemy forces and then helped in the evacuation of refugees and Service personnel.

Most of the craft were destroyed when Rangoon fell, marking the end of any Coastal Forces operations in South east Asia until the final Arakan campaign. Two MTB flotillas were formed at Madras and Trincomalee towards the end of 1942 to carry out patrol duties as part of the defence of India. But they saw no action, and because of rapid deterioration due to inadequate maintenance facilities, they were scrapped in 1944.

At the time when Japanese planes attacked Pearl Harbor on the morning of 7th December 1941, precipitating America's entry into the war, there were no more than twenty-nine PT boats in service with the US Navy. These were Elco seventy-seven-foot craft which had been formed into three MTB squadrons. The first, under Lieutenant-Commander William C Specht USN, was based at Pearl Harbor. As the bombs began to fall, the PT crews rushed to man their guns and managed to bring down two of the Japanese torpedo planes. None of the PTs were damaged, and after the raid they helped to ferry the wounded to hospital. Squadron 1 then remained at Pearl Harbor for the next six months, until they were sent to Midway.

Squadron 2, under Lieutenant-Commander Earl S Caldwell USN, was fitting out in the New York Navy Yard before being shipped some days later to Panama, where they helped to augment the defences of the Canal.

The first six boats of Squadron 3, under Lieutenant John D Bulkeley USN, were in Manila Bay, having arrived on 28th September. These were the first PTs to see combat, during the four-month struggle to defend the Philippines. It began three days after the Pearl Harbor attack with a heavy air raid on Manila. The PTs had managed to put out into the bay and by constant manoeuvring avoided the dive bombers, at the same time bringing down three of them by gunfire. But the Navy Yard was destroyed, together with much of the equipment and fuel for the PTs. So they moved to a new base at Sisiman Bay, at the end of Bataan Peninsula, and from there carried out nightly patrols during the rest of December while the US Asiatic Fleet withdrew to the south.

By the end of the month, when the US Army had withdrawn to Bataan and General Douglas MacArthur established headquarters on the island of Corregidor, the PTs were virtually the only US fighting craft left. Without spare parts and only a little fuel, they were rapidly deteriorating. The first casualty came on Christmas Day, when PT 33 ran aground on a coral reef after engine failure and had to be scuttled to prevent her falling into Japanese hands.

The remaining PTs fought back as well as they could. During a raid on Binanga Bay on the night of 18th January, PT 34, commanded by Bulkeley, torpedoed and sank a large merchant ship armed with 5.5-inch guns. PT 31 was to have taken part, but had been abandoned after setting out because of engine breakdown. Her crew managed to return to base the following day after paddling in two native canoes only yards from a beach where hundreds of Japanese troops were camped.

That left four boats. They continued to harass enemy shipping wherever they could, and on one occasion even scored a torpedo hit on a Japanese cruiser off the Bataan coast. But the

The Pacific and South-east Asian arena

Above left: Lieutenant-Commander
John D Bulkeley
Above right: Lieutenant
Robert B Kelly

relentless advance of Japanese forces made an evacuation from the Philippines inevitable. Early in March, General MacArthur and other senior officers were instructed to leave Corregidor.

It was intended that the first leg of their journey should be made by submarine, with the PTs as escorts. But from a sharp increase in the activities of enemy warships off Subic Bay, it was apparent that the Japanese Navy was intent on intercepting them. So the evacuation was put forward and made by PT boat instead. Bulkeley, with PT 41, took General and Mrs MacArthur, their son, and Major General Richard Sutherland, MacArthur's Chief of Staff; PT 35, commanded by Ensign Anthony Akers USNR, took Admiral Rockwell and his Chief of Staff, Captain Ray; and other passengers were taken by PT 34 (Lieutenant Robert Kelly USN) and PT 32 (Lieutenant (junior grade) Vincent Schumacher USN).

The four boats left in great secrecy and made rendezvous at the entrance to Manila Bay at 22 00hrs on 11th March. They faced a 560-mile voyage to Cagayan on Mindanas Island, for the

most part through Japanese patrolled waters. It was planned to hide up by day amongst the various islands and proceed only at night. The boats were to keep together, so that if one broke down her passengers could be transferred to the others.

But this proved impossible from the very start. Apart from suffering severe mechanical defects, the boats had to be stopped every hour or so to clean the carburettors of wax-contaminated gasoline. A strong easterly wind was blowing, which made the going very rough and put even greater strain on them. And a wide detour had to be made west of Mindoro Strait to avoid enemy warships which were waiting to cut them off.

By morning, in spite of all the efforts by their crews, the boats had become separated. Even though two hours late, PT 34 was the first to arrive at Taganayan Island, where the craft were to hide up during the daylight hours of 12th March. There was no sign of the others, and Kelly and his passengers spent an anxious day of waiting until, late in the afternoon, PTs 41 and 32 came creeping into the cove. Unable because of engine trouble to make the rendezvous in time, they had been hiding amongst other islands to avoid air attack and joined up on the way to Taganayan. But there was no sign of PT 35.

After a hurried conference and examination of the boats, it was obvious that PT 32 could not continue. She had lost most of her fuel, had only one engine working, and there were leaks in the hull. Her passengers were transferred to the other two boats and Schumacher directed to wait for PT 35 in case she arrived and then make independently for Cagayan.

As soon as it began to get dark, PT 34 and PT 41 left on what was to be the last stage of the journey to Cagayan. They had been on their way for less than an hour when a Japanese cruiser was suddenly sighted to the north. Luckily the PTs were hidden in the glare of the setting sun and the cruiser turned away without seeing them. Bulkeley cautiously led the boats from one island to another, keeping as close inshore as he dared. Soon after midnight a heavy storm blew up, drenching passengers and crews alike. But it helped the two boats to slip through the heavily patrolled waters, in which every Japanese ship was keeping a sharp lookout for them. On the morning of 13th March, they arrived safely at Cagayan after thirty-seven hours of continual danger from the enemy, the weather, and the boats themselves which were rapidly deteriorating. Several days later, General MacArthur and his party were flown to Australia, where he began the task of building up the force that was ultimately to return to liberate the Philippines.

Bulkeley was ordered to continue his attacks on enemy shipping for as long as the PTs lasted. There were only three of them left now. PT 35 had managed to reach Cagayan later on the 13th, but PT 32 had had to be scuttled when Schumacher found her no longer seaworthy. The crews worked valiantly to patch up the leaks and keep the faltering engines going, but at various times all three boats were out of action. Nevertheless, they kept up their harassment of the Japanese, who were now completing their occupation of the Philippines.

The last PT engagement was fought on the night of 8th April. Bulkeley in PT 41 and Kelly in PT 34 had made for the eastern side of Cebu to lie in wait for two enemy destroyers that had been reported heading through the Tanon Strait. But what emerged round the southern tip of the island was not two destroyers but a light cruiser, complete with 5.5-inch and 3-inch guns.

The PTs crept up to within 500 yards of the cruiser and fired their torpedoes. Bulkeley's first two missed, then the last two were seen to hit but failed to explode. Kelly's first two also missed astern, and before he could fire the others, his boat was caught in the beam of the cruiser's searchlight and came under heavy gunfire. The PT was riddled with holes and her mast shot away. Bulkeley moved in to attempt to draw the cruiser's fire while Kelly closed to within 300 yards and fired his last two torpedoes.

Turning away at maximum speed, Kelly suddenly found himself under fire from a destroyer which had loomed up to port. The cruiser turned and it looked as if the PT was trapped between the two ships. Then two spouts of water shot up amidships at the cruiser's waterline, the searchlight faded and her guns stopped firing. This gave Kelly a chance to escape. He joined Bulkeley and the two PTs made a run for shallow water south of Mindanao, where the destroyer which was chasing them could not follow.

Whether the torpedoes had struck the cruiser or whether, as Kelly first thought, she had been hit by shells from the Japanese destroyer, was never known. Japanese reports indicate merely that the cruiser, which was the 5,000-ton *Kuma*, was hit by torpedoes which failed to explode. Whatever the damage actually caused, she remained afloat until 11th January 1944, when she was sunk by a British submarine off Penang.

Later that night, while Kelly was trying to reach Cebu City to obtain

Subic
Bay

Bataan
Pen

Manila

Binanga
Bay

*Manila
Bay*

Manila

LUZON

Sisiman Bay

Corregidor

Lagu
de B

LUZON

Manila

**PHILIPPINE
ISLANDS**

MINDORO

PACIFIC

OCEAN

SAMAR

Tañon
Str.

PANAY

LEYTE

Tagauayan I

NEGROS

CEBU

PALAWAN

13 th MARCH
PT 34, 35 & 41
ARRIVE

SULU

SEA

Cagayan

MINDANAO

Davao

0   Miles   100

0   Kilometres   20

The Philippines; MacArthur's route from Manila to Cagayan

medical aid for the wounded, his boat was bombed by Japanese aircraft. One plane was brought down, but PT 34 was set on fire and exploded after beaching. Two of the crew were killed, but Kelly managed to get the rest, including the wounded, ashore. The two remaining PTs, their careers as torpedo boats ended as there were no more torpedoes available, were scuttled a few days later as the Japanese entered Cebu.

Bulkeley was later awarded the Medal of Honor and the Navy Cross for his exploits during the four months before the final fall of the Philippines – Kelly and Ensign Cox USN, the first officer of PT 41, receiving the Navy Cross. On 13th April, under orders from General MacArthur, Bulkeley was flown to Australia. On his return to the United States he brought with him a message from MacArthur which stressed the effectiveness of motor torpedo boats in coastal waters of the Pacific islands and the need for them to be formed into a separate arm of the service. MacArthur wanted 200 boats made available within eight months. His request was not fulfilled in that period of time, but it was the start of the build-up of a motor torpedo boat force that eventually totalled some 300 PTs.

Before a return could be made to the Philippines, American and Commonwealth forces had to fight their way across the other Pacific territories that had been overrun by the Japanese. This resolved itself into two great campaigns; that fought by the South Pacific Force in the Solomon Islands, and by the Southwest Pacific Force in New Guinea. PT boats played a vital part in both, but it was not until October 1942 that they saw action again, following the US landings on Guadalcanal in August.

Meanwhile, the US Navy concentrated on developing the types of boats that would be needed. There was much to do, not only in the actual construction of large numbers of boats but in training crews, commissioning squadrons and the PT tenders to be used for servicing and communications, and forming mobile bases that could be rapidly set up and dismantled with equipment carried by the PTs themselves. Such bases would be essential in the wide-ranging war that was to be fought in the Pacific, particularly with the kind of island-hopping strategy that was envisaged. All this was a new element in US naval warfare, just as Coastal Forces had been to the Royal Navy. But at least the experience of men like Bulkeley, who had already fought in PTs, could be called upon. And studies were made of the motor torpedo boat warfare that was raging in the narrow seas off the British Isles.

The nearest that the PTs came to any action during this period was during the Battle of Midway. The boats of Squadron 1 had been ordered to proceed to Midway under their own power at the end of May – a voyage of 1,385 miles that was the longest ever made across open water by PTs and accomplished successfully with only one boat having to turn back through mechanical failure.

On the morning of 4th June, shortly after their arrival, the Japanese launched an air attack on Midway. But this time the Americans were prepared. While the PTs helped to hold off the low-flying dive bombers, US aircraft from Midway and the carriers of the US Pacific Fleet were blasting the Japanese invasion fleet far to the north-west. By the end of the day the Japanese were routed, suffering such naval losses they they could no longer hold out any hope of expanding their conquests eastward. Just before midnight the PTs were ordered out to search for any damaged Japanese carriers that might have broken away from where the great sea battle had taken place. But the weather was bad, with poor visibility, and although they searched all night the boats made no contact with the enemy. Only floating wreckage could be seen.

Torpedo war in the Mediterranean

The Battle of the Mediterranean was one of the key factors in denying the Axis powers ultimate victory and in giving the Allies time to prepare and launch the Second Front. The outcome depended largely on sea power as both sides fought to keep open the supply routes to their land forces, while at the same time trying to cut off those of the opposition. It was a battle in which small craft of all types, employed in large numbers by all the major powers, had a vital part to play.

There was much greater scope for small boat warfare in the Mediterranean. The Germans and Italians used motor torpedo boats to attack Malta and other British bases; to attack not only merchant shipping as in the North Sea but warships as well, including cruisers. British, Commonwealth and American boats carried out the same kind of operations but also took part in Commando raids, assisted partisan forces operat-

ing behind enemy lines, and in fact in a complex and constantly changing situation, they were used in as many different ways as their ingenious commanders could devise.

It was not until 1943 that the role of motor torpedo boats in this conflict began in earnest. By that time the fight for the narrow seas off Britain had also reached its peak, with the MGBs gradually gaining ascendancy over the German S-boats. Increasing numbers of craft were sent to the Mediterranean, together with commanders and crews who had already learned the technique of small boat fighting in the North Sea and English Channel.

While the larger warships of the British, German and Italian fleets battled for supremacy in the deeper waters of the Mediterranean and merchant ship convoys ran the gauntlet to get supplies through, motor torpedo boat operations were in

Left: **Taking the salute on leaving base.** *Above:* **Higgins type PT at speed**

general tied more closely to those of the land forces. They began off the North African coast, then moved up to Sicily and Italy and extended to the Aegean, the Adriatic, and off the southern coast of France.

After the fall of France and Italy's entry into the war in June 1940, it was not long before all those countries which had remained neutral were held by the Axis. They controlled the entire northern coastline from France to the Balkans, including Greece and Crete, and the southern coastline from Algeria to the Egyptian border. Only Egypt, Palestine, and Gibraltar, Malta and Cyprus were in British hands. The Italian Fleet greatly outnumbered that of the British, which had been depleted for operations elsewhere in home and Atlantic waters, and this was particularly so in the case of motor torpedo boats. Against over 100 Italian MAS boats

based in the Adriatic, the Aegean, the Red Sea and along the North African coast, all that the British could muster were nine of the old type fifty-five-foot Thornycroft MTBs that had been building for the Finnish and Philippine navies and which had been hastily shipped to Alexandria and formed into the 10th MTB Flotilla; the 1st MTB Flotilla of BPB boats having been brought back from Malta to home waters at the end of 1939.

Soon after the arrival of the Thornycroft boats, five of them were sent to help in the defence of Crete. They suffered continually from engine breakdowns and a lack of fuel supplies. And then, during a German air attack on Suda Bay on 23rd May 1941, all five were destroyed.

The four remaining boats were used mainly for patrol work in the harbours of Alexandria and Haifa. But the value of such craft was by then well appreciated, and large numbers were urgently requested for use in the Mediterranean. The Admiralty had

93

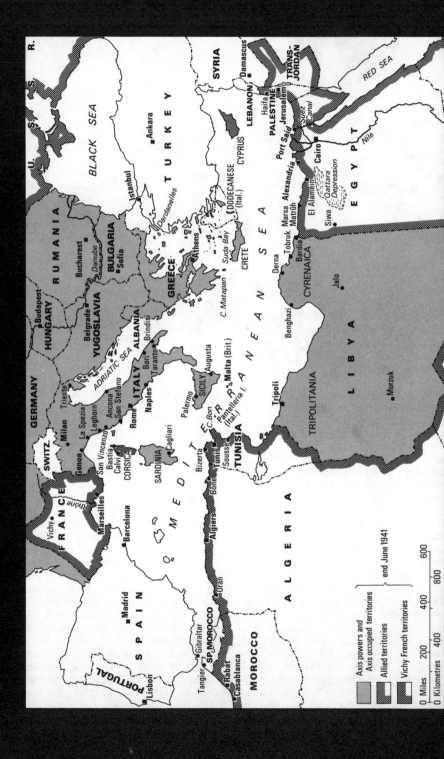

none to spare from home waters, where they were desperately trying to cope at this time with the German S-boat menace, but fortunately boats were made available from two other sources. The Canadian Government offered to supply twelve of the seventy-foot BPB craft they were building, and arrangements were made under lend-lease for two flotillas of ten boats each of American Elcos to be transferred to the Royal Navy in the Mediterranean. By the time these were available early in 1942, the rapid building programme in Britain also made it possible for MTBs, MGBs and MLs to be allocated to this theatre, together with trained British, Canadian, and Commonwealth crews. And so the build-up of Coastal Forces in the Mediterranean began.

The overall situation in Mediterranean waters had undergone violent fluctuations. Italy's entry into the conflict, with her impressive fleet and large submarine force, had posed a serious threat. But it was one which did not fully materialise, firstly because the Italian fleet showed itself unwilling to engage in battle, enabling the British to retain the initiative even with outnumbered forces, and secondly because the Italians were unable to take control of Malta, which became even more vital as an air base than as a naval base. Although Britain was denied an open sea route through the Mediterranean, except for occasional fast military convoys, and most of her supplies to Egypt had to go the long way round the Cape, the strategic situation by the end of 1940 was by no means unfavourable. There was good hope that the Italians could be pushed out of Libya and East Africa the following year.

This changed abruptly early in 1941 with the intervention of German forces in the Mediterranean theatre. The Luftwaffe, based in Sicily, began a devastating onslaught against Malta and on British shipping. German troops arriving in Greece forced the eventual evacuation of British forces from there at the end of April and from Crete at the end of May, giving the Axis control of the Aegean and the approaches to the Dardanelles. And the arrival of Rommel's *Afrika Korps* in Libya resulted in the British Army falling back to a besieged position in Tobruk.

Although the Italian fleet as a whole had been unwilling to engage in battle, this certainly did not apply to their small boat forces. MAS boats based on the island of Pantellaria had made a number of successful attacks on Malta-bound convoys. On 20th June they sunk the submarine *Union* of the Malta flotilla, and the following month, together with aircraft, MAS boats took part in a heavy attack on Malta itself. It was only through the alertness of the island defences that they were beaten off.

In addition to helping their Italian allies in so many other ways, the Germans decided in 1941 to send S-boats to the Mediterranean. Their specific purpose was to support the attack from the sea that was to be Operation Hercules – the invasion and conquest of Malta, that for so long had been a thorn in the side of the Axis powers.

The first to be transferred was the 3rd S-boat Flotilla which, under the command of *Korvettenkapitän* F Kemnade and including *Kapitänleutnant* Siegfried Wuppermann as a group commander, had been operating in the English Channel. The journey via German and French canals to the Mediterranean was made in great secrecy – the boats were disguised with dummy funnels and superstructure to look like tugs – and ironically followed part of the same route that had been travelled by the British MTBs when returning from Malta to the English Channel at the end of 1939.

At La Spezia, the boats were converted back to their normal shape and colours and then sailed for Sicily, where they were based at Augusta and arrived in time for the concerted drive against Malta in the early months of 1942.

Above: One of the American Elco PTs transferred to the Royal Navy.
Below: MTB 265 being towed stern first after a fight in the Messina Straits

This period saw the Allied situation in the Mediterranean at its lowest ebb. The only bright spot in the picture had been the defeat of the Italian forces in East Africa and the shattering of Mussolini's dream of creating an East African Empire. But it did little to compensate for the British defeats elsewhere.

While the Luftwaffe increased the intensity of its attacks on Malta and U-boats created havoc amongst the convoys that were desperately trying to keep the garrison supplied, the first main task of the S-boats, working with the Italian MAS boats, was to lay mines. It was only sixty miles from the southern tip of Sicily to La Valetta, a distance that the boat could easily cover in two hours.

But in spite of the overwhelming forces mounted against her, Malta was not subdued. The Malta-based Spitfires, although few in number, took a heavy toll of the attackers. As in the English Channel the S-boats found themselves vulnerable to air attack by day and had to operate only at night. And increasingly they had to postpone mine-laying operations in order to rescue Luftwaffe pilots whose planes had been brought down in the sea between Malta and Sicily.

In May the S-boat flotilla was moved to a new base at Derna, thirty-five miles west of the British garrison at Tobruk, to patrol the waters off the North African coast through which supplies were arriving in preparation for Rommel's big offensive. And the following month, on 14th June, they scored the first major motor torpedo boat success in the Mediterranean. A large British convoy had set out from Alexandria, heavily escorted, to try to get supplies through to Malta. It was spotted by German aircraft and Wuppermann was ordered to intercept and attack with five S-boats. His first attempt, shortly before midnight, was beaten off by the destroyer escorts, and by the time his force had regrouped he had lost contact with the convoy. That might have been the end of the story, but several hours later, hearing that the superior Italian battle fleet had put out from Taranto to intercept the convoy, the British ships turned on a reverse course in the hope of throwing the Italians off the scent. As chance would have it, this brought them exactly back to the area in which the S-boats had been searching unsuccessfully to find them.

Wuppermann, in S-56, suddenly found himself in the middle of a group of British destroyers and a cruiser. During the following engagement, he torpedoed and seriously damaged the cruiser, which was the 9,000-ton Southampton class *Newcastle*, and another of the S-boats damaged one of the destroyers so badly that she had to be sunk by a consort.

By this time, the first British Coastal Forces base had been established at Alexandria and the American and Canadian boats formed into the 10th and 15th MTB Flotillas, under such experienced officers as Lieutenant-Commander C S D Noakes RN, Lieutenant Dennis Jermain RN, and Lieutenant Robert Allan RNVR. Their first operations were in patrolling the waters off Tobruk, helping to keep the garrison there supplied, and 'false-nose jobs' (as clandestine operations were called), such as landing agents on enemy-held Crete.

The fall of Tobruk put Rommel's forces just two day march from Alexandria. But the British line was held at El Alamein, and Rommel, starved of petrol and equipment due to the continued attacks by the Royal Navy and Malta-based planes of the RAF against his supply routes, was unable to make his final armoured thrust into Egypt.

His defeat in the last battle of El Alamein at the end of October was helped by the MTBs, who made a feint sea-borne landing sixty miles to the west to mislead the Germans into thinking they were being attacked in force behind their lines and cause a diversion of their troops. The MTBs closed the beaches on the night of the

23rd and simulated a landing by sending up showers of tracer, dropping lights and smoke-floats in the water, and broadcasting a variety of noises over loudspeakers to give the impression of large bodies of troops going ashore. The plan was a complete success, and although the MTBs were later attacked from the air, they suffered only minor damage.

By the beginning of 1943, Coastal Forces had been built up to four flotillas of MTBs, seven of MLs, and eight of HDMLs. The MTBs were then amalgamated into two main flotillas, the 7th (Lieutenant R A Hennessy RN) and the 10th (Lieutenant Jermain), both operating from Malta. Amongst their successes was the sinking of the Italian submarine *Santorre Santorosa*. But they played little part in the main event at the end of 1942, which was Operation Torch, the American and British landings in French North Africa.

While the Allied forces pressed on towards the great naval bases at Tunis and Bizerta, from where they would later be able to launch an assault on Sicily and Italy, the 10th MTB Flotilla was ordered to Bône, on the Tunisian coast one hundred miles west of Bizerta. Originally intended as a temporary base, this became the main Coastal Forces headquarters and repair centre until after the invasion of Italy.

In command at Bône was Robert Allan, who was largely responsible for building up Coastal Forces in the Mediterranean. Before the end of the year he had been promoted to Lieutenant-Commander, at twenty-eight the youngest in the RNVR. His many decorations included the DSO, OBE, Croix de Guerre, Legion of Honour, the American Legion of Merit, and several Mentions in Despatches.

The MTBs which still operated from Malta meanwhile switched their area of operations to the east coast of Sicily and off the island of Pantelleria, where most of the German and Italian motor torpedo boats were now based.

In view of the extra distance they had to travel, the boats were fitted with extra fuel tanks on their decks. Their most successful operations at this time were in laying mines in the routes through which the Axis convoys were trying to get supplies to Tunisia.

April saw an even greater build-up of Coastal Forces. The first of the 'D' type Fairmiles arrived, together with more Vosper and Elco MTBs. And a squadron of American Higgins-type PTs, number 15, under Lieutenant Commander Stanley M Barnes USN, was sent to Bône, where they came under the overall command of British Coastal Forces. These PTs, later reinforced by other squadrons, were for some time the only US Navy craft operating in the Mediterranean.

By this time, Allan's MTBs were beginning to score successes against what were to be their most persistent targets in the Mediterranean – the heavily armed German F-lighters which were used for transporting fuel and supplies. As the Germans had already found with their boats, the MTBs had to operate mainly at night for the Luftwaffe still controlled the waters between Sicily and Tunisia. As an experiment, it was decided to try using the MTBs in daylight. The man chosen for this hazardous task was Stewart Gould, fresh from his achievements in MGBs in the English Channel and now commanding the new 32nd MTB Flotilla at Bône.

Gould left Bône on the night of 25th April with two MTBs, intending to go up the coast to Sousse to meet up with two more craft which were to take part in the mission. But during what was meant to be a routine passage, he came across two F-lighters in Bizerta Bay. He attacked them with torpedoes, then when these missed, as they usually did by running underneath the shallow-draft lighters, he attacked with guns. Both of the enemy craft caught fire and sank.

Two days later, in full daylight, the four MTBs were patrolling along the Tunisian coast. The enemy were taken

Top: **The Italian motor torpedo boat MAS 562, captured by PT boats on 30th June 1944.** *Above:* **An MTB leaves Leghorn harbour on patrol**

completely by surprise at seeing the 'night-hunters' out by day. Two Italian minesweepers and a German R-boat were attacked and sunk, then the MTBs strafed several Junkers transport planes on the beach and brought down another as it came in to land.

So far the mission had been a great success. Then shortly after midday the MTBs sighted an enemy convoy with a heavy air escort. Gould ordered an attack, but before the MTBs could get close, they were themselves attacked by aircraft. Gould's boat was destroyed and he himself was killed. The other boats only just managed to get away, using their high speed to manoeuvre out of the way of the aircraft and the shore batteries which had by now joined in.

The first success for the PTs came on the night of 8th May, when Barnes in PT 206 sank an Italian merchant ship

off Cape Bon. This marked the beginning of many successful joint operations by American and British boats, in which the PTs had the advantage of being equipped with radar which enabled them to locate enemy ships more easily, while the MTBs, for the first twelve months or so, possessed rather more reliable torpedoes for making an attack.

These tactics culminated in the spring of 1944 in the formation by Commander Allan of a special Coastal Forces Battle Squadron, the most spectacular and successful small boat unit of the war. By this time the Allied armies had completed the occupation of Sicily, had landed in Southern Italy, after which the Italians had surrendered, and were driving the Germans up the Italian mainland. The British and American boats had taken an active part in all these operations and were now operating in three distinct areas – off the west coast of Italy, in the Adriatic, and in the Aegean.

Allan was in command of operations in the western area, where one flotilla

For over a year, PT s were the only US Navy craft in the Mediterranean. Crew at battle stations

each of 'D'-type MTBs and MGBs and the American PTs under Barnes were based at Bastia, in Corsica, from where they could patrol the entire Gulf of Genoa. As the German supply lines by road and rail came under continual air attack, they were relying increasingly on waterborne transport from the north. This mainly took the form of F-lighters and cargo ships that made the run down the coast by night behind protective minefields and under cover of shore batteries. These made it too risky to send in destroyers to stop the traffic, and so it became the job of the small boats of Coastal Forces.

Experience had shown that torpedoes usually passed underneath the shallow-draught lighters, and that

strongly built as the enemy craft were, it was extremely difficult to sink them by gunfire. The arrival of the MGBs with their 6-pounder guns helped, but even so the lighters were themselves equipped with 8-inch and 6-inch guns which made them powerful adversaries in a gun battle.

And so Allan devised his Battle Squadron. The Battle Group comprised three British LCGs (Landing Craft Guns), each mounting two 4.7-inch and two 40mm guns. These were screened from possible S-boat attack by an Escort Group, made up of MGBs and MTBs. In the van of the Squadron was a Scouting Group of PTs, which were to search ahead for possible targets and also act as a screen against enemy destroyers in the vicinity. And finally there was the Control Group, also of PTs, from which Allan commanded the whole operation.

One of the Squadron's most success-

l operations took place on the
ght of 24th April 1944. Allan led the
ontrol Group in PT 218, with PT 209,
he Scouting Group of PTs 202, 212,
nd 213 were led by Lieutenant Edwin
u Bose USNR. The Battle Group of
CGs 14, 19 and 20 were escorted by
Ts 211 and 216, MTBs 633, 640 and 655,
nd MGBs 657, 660 and 662. The MTBs
ere commanded by Lieutenant-Com-
ander Tim Bligh RNVR, and the
GBs by Lieutenant-Commander
ouglas Maitland RCNVR. These
nboats were from the 56th Flotilla
n which every boat was commanded
y a Canadian, including such veteran
ommanders as Cornelius Burke and
homas Ladner who had come over to
ngland early on in the war as volun-
ers to serve in Coastal Forces, first
f all fighting in small boats off the
asts of Britain and now in the
editerranean.

The force left Bastia at different
mes in the afternoon because of
eir different speeds and made ren-
zvous in the vicinity of Vada Rocks
2000hrs. At just about this time a
erman convoy of eight F-lighters
d a tug was setting off from Leghorn
take supplies down the coast to San
tefano, and a smaller convoy of two
awlers, each towing a barge, was
rthward bound on its way back to
eghorn.

Radar contact was made with both
nvoys soon after 2200hrs as their
ths began to converge. Allan decided
attack the main group first. Within
inutes four of the lighters and the
g had been sunk by the LCGs. The
GBs found a fifth lighter abandoned
d sank her by gunfire. Then the
CGs located the three remaining
ghters. Two were hit and sunk
most immediately, but the third,
ter returning a high rate of fire
hich only just missed the LCGs, drew
vay damaged under cover of a heavy
nokescreen. The MTBs were sent to
nish her off, but although they did
flict further damage the craft did not
nk and eventually beached south of
n Vincenzo.

Some while later the Scouting Group
made contact with the northbound
convoy. The LCGs were too far away
to make an interception, so the PTs
made an attack with torpedoes. One
of the trawlers was sunk, but the
other opened heavy fire which forced
the PTs to withdraw under a smoke-
screen.

The Battle Squadron was then
ordered to return to Bastia, only to
find their path blocked by three
German destroyers which appeared
to be waiting to intercept them but
were in fact laying mines. They were
engaged by the PTs of the Scouting
Group, who fired their remaining
torpedoes. One of the destroyers, TA
23, was damaged by an explosion.
Whether it was the result of a torpedo
hit or striking a mine is not known,
but she was so badly damaged that she
had to be sunk later by one of the
other German craft.

No further contact with the enemy
was made. All the Allied boats returned
without damage or casualties, having
sunk ten enemy craft and severely
damaged another.

In May, the original PT Squadron
15 was reinforced by the arrival of two
more, Squadrons 22 and 29. The
American boats, under Lieutenant-
Commander Barnes who had been
awarded the Navy Cross for his
heroism and leadership during the
Tunisian and Sicilian campaigns,
operated from two bases in Corsica at
Bastia and Calvi. Equipped with
better torpedoes which could be fired
from light racks instead of through
heavy torpedo-tubes and mounting
40mm guns, they were now far more
effective. Within three months,
operating alone, they claimed two
corvettes, eleven F-lighters, one cargo
ship and several small craft sunk, and
one MAS boat captured. Further craft
were sunk in joint operations with
British craft. Then, on 1st August, the
PTs were withdrawn from operations
to prepare for the part they were to
play in the invasion of Southern
France, scheduled for 15th August.

Hide and seek among the islands

Following the Allied landing in Italy in September 1943, Allan had taken his boats to operate off the west coast of Italy while other MTBs and MGBs began operations in the Aegean and Adriatic.

The key to the situation in the Aegean was Turkey. If the Allies could hold the islands and control the Aegean shipping routes, it was hoped that Turkey might be brought into the war on the Allied side. British garrisons were established on Leros, Kalimno, Symi and several other islands in September and plans were made to land on Rhodes, the gateway to the Dodecanese.

But the Germans were equally determined not to let the Aegean go to the Allies. Large forces of troops, vessels for seaborne operations and aircraft were moved to Greece and the Germans forestalled the British by themselves capturing Rhodes on 13th September. They quickly took over a number of the other islands, then moved against those held by the British. With the Luftwaffe dominant

in the skies, most of the Briti[garrisons fell one by one, ending wi[the surrender of Leros on 16[November.

Without sufficient forces availab[the Allies had to give up their plan f[control of the Aegean. Operatio[from this point on were confined [small-scale Commando raids a[guerilla warfare by resistance group mainly with the intention of keepi[as many German forces as possib[tied down in the area so that th[could not go to reinforce the ma[battle taking place in Italy. It was t[kind of hit-and-run warfare in whic[Coastal Forces had a prominent pa[to play. Many of the smaller islan[were not garrisoned by either sid[and could be used by the MTBs [hideouts during the day, while [night they set out to attack enen[shipping and took part in vario[raids. Some of the lightly garrison[islands changed hands several tim[as they were raided first by one sid[then the other.

The 10th MTB Flotilla under Lie[

enant-Commander Peter Evensen RN, made up of the older Elco boats that had been transferred to the Royal Navy under lend-lease, moved into the Aegean in October to operate from an advanced base on the island of Casteloriso, where the British maintained a small garrison. From here they carried out night patrols among the enemy-held islands, attacking lighters, tugs and small caiques which the Germans used for bringing in supplies, and maintaining contact with Greek agents and resistance leaders.

Typical of the Combined Operations raids carried out during this period was an attack on the German garrison on Symi in July 1944. Eight MLs, four HDMLs, two schooners and MTB 309 transported the 224 British and Greek troops who took part. While they captured the enemy garrison and destroyed the ammunition dumps and island defences, the boat kept up a bombardment from offshore and sank one Italian MAS boat and captured another. Within twenty-four hours the Allied force had departed. The Germans re-occupied the island and began the laborious task of building up new defences.

The MLs which had taken part were amongst a number assigned to Aegean Raiding Operations earlier in the year from Alexandria. Together with the MTBs they were also responsible for sinking a number of enemy craft and keeping up this kind of guerilla warfare, in which the Germans never knew when or where the Allies would strike next.

Eventually, after the landings in Normandy and Southern France, the Germans were compelled in August to begin evacuating the Aegean. As the Greek islands were liberated, a Coastal Force base was established on Kithera and more craft arrived from other Mediterranean areas. Many of their activities from then on until the liberation of Athens were concerned with cloak-and-dagger missions to aid the partisans.

Similar operations, only conducted on a larger scale, took place in the Adriatic. Coastal Forces had first moved into this area at the end of 1943, their original purpose being to attack enemy shipping along the east coast of Italy. Two MTB flotillas were based first of all at Brindisi and then further up the coast at Bari. But they found fewer targets than they had expected.

It was at this time that the Allies took the decision to help Marshal Tito's partisan forces who were fighting a guerilla war in Yugoslavia and keeping as many as fifteen German divisions contained in the Balkan Peninsula. Commando parties, agents and supplies had to be brought across the Adriatic from Italy into Greece, Albania and Yugoslavia, a task which was given to Special Service MLs. The MTBs in the meantime had found heavier concentrations of enemy coastal shipping off Dalmatia than along the Italian east coast, and so their main activities were transferred to this new area at the end of the year.

Advanced Coastal Forces bases were established on the islands of Vis and Hvar. As in the other Mediterranean areas the Luftwaffe held command of the skies by day, so that the boats operated mostly at night, hiding up under camouflage during the daylight hours among the islands.

Successful attacks on enemy landing craft and lighters came quickly, and on 21st December the MTBs achieved their biggest single success by sinking the ex-Yugoslavian cruiser *Dalmatia*, which had been taken over by the Germans and renamed *Niobe*, off Silba Island.

This did something to mitigate a disaster earlier in the month at the main Coastal Force base at Bari when, during a sudden raid by German aircraft, a convoy of seventeen cargo ships which had just arrived was destroyed. A number of MTBs which were tied up at the jetty at the time were also seriously damaged, but the greatest blow was the fact that

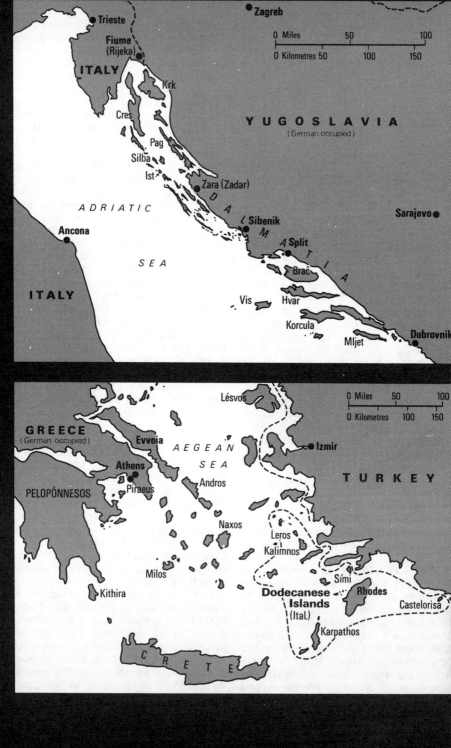

...ongst the cargoes destroyed were ...w Packard engines and spare parts ... the MTB flotillas.

...Because of this depletion in the ...ength of Coastal Forces in the ...riatic, arrangements were made to ...ng reinforcements in from Allan's ...tillas on the west coast of Italy. ...ese included 'D'-type MGBs from ... 61st Flotilla, together with its ...nadian Senior Officer, Lieutenant-...mmander Tom Fuller RCNVR.

...s Coastal Forces activity along the ...lmatian coast increased, the ...rmans decided that it was necessary ...occupy the islands that were giving ...elter to the boats, as they had done ...the Aegean. In the face of much ...ger forces, the British Commandos ...l the partisans withdrew from their ...risons. Only Vis was held in ...ength, because of its importance as ...oastal Forces base, as a terminal ...nt for the delivery of arms to Tito, ...l as a springboard for any large-...le operations which might be found ...essary in the Balkans.

...he Germans proceeded to occupy a ...mber of the Dalmatian islands, ...luding Korcula, Brac and Hvar. But ...en it came to the question of ...acking Vis, a bitter quarrel broke ... between the German army and ...val commands as to who should be ...marily responsible for the opera-...n. This led to a postponement of ... intended attack, first to March ...l then to April.

...t was during this time that Fuller ...vised a new and remarkable form of ...ack with his MGBs. They had ...eady begun to find lucrative targets ...the schooners which the Germans ...re using for coastal transportation ...l several of these had been sunk in ...rch by the boats based at Vis. On ... night of 2nd April Fuller set out ...h two boats, MTB 651 (Lieutenant ...M Horlock RNVR) and MGB 647 ...eutenant Mountstevens RNVR), on ...ission to the Dalmatian coast to

pick up four American special agents who had an Italian prisoner with them. Fuller was on board the MTB.

This part of the operation was carried out successfully. It had then been Fuller's intention to enter Zulana Harbour to strafe the German garrison there, but he was warned by the American agents that the Germans had recently moved in 155mm and anti-tank batteries. So instead he proceeded along the coast east of Zulana.

After a while, a small schooner was sighted. The normal procedure would have been to challenge her, take the crew prisoner, and then sink the craft by gunfire. But Fuller had other ideas. The base at Vis was short of certain supplies. It seemed a pity to waste those that the schooner was obviously carrying. So he brought his boat up close, boarded the enemy craft, over-powered her crew, and took her under tow back to Vis. The cargo was found to include explosives, land mines, engineering equipment and cigarettes, all intended for the German garrison at Korcula.

The following night, Fuller set out with the same two boats and this time brought back two enemy schooners, adding cargoes of wheat and ammuni-tion to the booty of the previous night.

These exploits set a new pattern of operations. The other boats eagerly joined in the hunt and it became vir-tually a competition as to who could bring in the biggest prizes. In the month of April alone, four boats from Vis captured no less than eight schooners with their cargoes intact and a lighter and a motor boat, in addition to sink-ing several other craft which showed no inclination to surrender. The captured vessels were turned over to the partisans, who normally accom-panied the MTBs and MGBs to navigate amongst the islands and whose piratical and blood-curdling shouts when closing with the enemy usually ensured a minimum of resistance. The vessels were then armed and added to

...tish operations in the Eastern ...diterranean

the 'Tiger' fleet of the partisans.

As one Admiralty chief commented: 'The tactics evolved date from the 18th century and earlier and are evidently as effective now as then. It is clear that, to be consistently successful, the piratical tactics adopted require good seamanship and a high standard of co-operation between commanding officers and crews of the flotilla boats, together with complete confidence in the Senior Officer.'

Fuller was awarded a second Bar to his DSC for these actions, which were not always as easy as they seemed. There was always a dangerous moment when about to board that the enemy might be using the vessel as a decoy in order to attack the Coastal Forces craft while lying stopped, their most vulnerable position. Later, after other flotillas in the Adriatic had also gone into the piracy business, there was a challenge to see who could achieve the minimum time to capture a vessel and have her in tow at ten knots. Fuller won, with a record time of twelve minutes.

As the boats from Vis began seriously to affect the enemy's coastal traffic, Admiral Dönitz, Commander-in-Chief of the German Navy, became even more insistent that the island should be seized. The Wehrmacht by this time were doubtful if it was worth the commitment of forces needed so badly elsewhere, and were not even convinced that they could continue to hold the island afterwards. The arguments were presented to Hitler. Although he agreed with Dönitz about the strategic importance of Vis, he felt that if the Army lacked conviction about the undertaking, it was not worth doing. And so the operation was called off, and Coastal Forces retained the base from which they were able to continue their night-hunting activities among the Dalmatian islands.

During the middle of June, further boats arrived at Vis from the west coast of Italy – the 57th MTB/MGB Flotilla of 'Dogs', as the Fairmiles

were called, under their new co manding officer, Lieutenant– Co mander Tim Bligh. They celebrat their arrival a few nights later sinking the German torpedo-boat which had been patrolling the Adria for some time, eluding previc attempts to find and engage her.

The next flotilla to arrive in Adriatic was the Canadian 56th, un Lieutenant – Commander Doug Maitland, fresh from its trium with Allan's 'Battle Squadron'. T was in July, at the same time that Germans began to use the heav armed F-lighters in the Adriatic in attempt to get supplies past marauding Dog-boats, which w now operating as combined MTBs a MGBs. Bligh was the first to co across these craft, while on patrol on the night of 7th August. His th boats intercepted two of the light off Vir Island.

Knowing how difficult it was torpedo the enemy craft, Bligh deci initially to make a gun attack. doing so, one of the lighters was set fire, but his own boat, MGB 662, also badly damaged, with one n killed and nine wounded. Then M 670 turned and fired a torpedo wh hit the second lighter. She became first boat in the Mediterranean sink a moving F-lighter by torpe The other lighter was eventua finished off by further gunfire.

Shortly afterwards, on the nigh the 17th, the Canadian MGBs had th first chance against the F-light Three of the boats, commanded Maitland, Burke and Ladner, sighte large convoy of lighters, schoon landing-craft and S-boats in the jet Channel. In a running gun bat two schooners, one S-boat, a ligh and a landing-craft were sunk four other vessels, including anot lighter, damaged. The MGBs got av virtually unscathed.

But the most successful action ca on the night of 11th October, by wh time the Germans were withdraw both from the Dalmatian islands

from Greece and the Aegean islands. It was in fact one of the most decisive Coastal Forces actions fought anywhere.

Four 'D'-boats under Bligh's command had left Vis on the afternoon of the 10th to patrol off the island of Zara and with the intention of lying up the following day at Ist Island. The first part of the mission was uneventful, but on arriving at Ist, Bligh was informed by the local partisan leader that an enemy convoy was expected to leave Zara northbound on the following night.

During the daylight hours of the 11th, the four boats remained in hiding as planned, and then set out to lie in wait for the convoy off Vir Light. Visibility was poor, and it came as a shock when shortly after 2300hrs Bligh suddenly sighted the convoy to seaward of his port bow at only 400 yards range. It appeared to comprise four F-lighters with an escorting flak-lighter, bristling with a quadruple 20mm aft, many 20mm guns in sponsons down the starboard side, and an 88mm amidships.

The range narrowed so quickly as the enemy craft bore down on the 'D'-boats that they were too close to fire torpedoes. A gun attack was ordered instead. Meanwhile, the flak-lighter had already opened fire, hitting two of the boats. MTB 634 (Lieutenant

Tim Bligh (left) on the bridge of MTB 662 with Able Seaman Stone, Petty Officer Briddon, Captain Stevens (commander of Coastal Forces in the Western Mediterranean), Tommy Ladner, and S Turner

Walter Blount DSC, RNVR) caught fire when her ammunition locker exploded, and one of the gunners on MTB 662 (Bligh's own craft) was killed. Then the guns from both boats raked the lighter, which burst into flames from stem to stern. Her bridge collapsed and as her ammunition exploded, she broke in two.

While the flames on MTB 634 were being put out, Bligh drew ahead and found himself engaging a host of targets off his port side. The gunfire was intense as these craft were also engaged by the other two boats, MTB 638 (Lieutenant D Lummis RNVR) and MTB 637 (Lieutenant R C Davidson DSC, RNVR). It was now apparent that there were many more enemy boats than the five lighters originally sighted, including landing-craft and S-boats which had obviously been escorting the convoy. Smoke was everywhere and the action was fought at such close range, often less than fifty yards, that it was impossible to see exactly what was happening.

After about ten minutes, those enemy craft that were still afloat drew away, leaving the burning wrecks of at least six boats and two upturned hulls behind them. The 'D'-boats began a sweep to the west and south in order to cut off any of the enemy that might try to return to Zara. During the next four hours they engaged further craft at sea and others that had beached along the coast. The destruction of these was completed with torpedoes. When eventually the D-boats turned to head back for Ist at 0400hrs, they left a trail of burning craft that were continually blowing up as their ammunition exploded.

When all the reports were put together and assessed, it became apparent that the four boats between them had sunk six F-lighters, four landing-craft and one S-boat; probably sunk another F-lighter; and damaged three S-boats, with one of them possibly sunk. Their own casualties were one killed, two seriously and one slightly wounded, and slight damage to MTBs 634 and 638. What actually happened was that by chance, the D-boats had come upon two enemy convoys, one from Sibenik and the other from Zara, at just the point where their paths crossed. In spite of the 6-pounder guns of the D-boats which had caused so much of the destruction, they had in fact been outnumbered by the great number of 88mm and 20mm guns possessed by the enemy. It was a remarkable achievement, made possible as the official report stated by low visibility, land background, uncertainty of identification by the enemy, absurdly close ranges, excellent gunnery, and admirable coolness on the part of the commanding officers.

Meanwhile, in the western waters of the Mediterranean, the PT squadrons had been taking part in Operation Dragoon, the Allied assault on southern France, together with support from British flotillas. The landings in August were a complete success, and it was only towards the end of the month that PTs and MTBs came into direct action with the enemy in the invasion area. This was

against the 'human torpedoes' an motor boats loaded with explosive that the Germans in desperatio launched in large numbers against th Allied supply ships. With the help o air patrols, the British and America boats located and destroyed most o them before they even had a chance o approaching the supply routes.

With this danger out of the way, th Allied boats resumed their patrols i the Gulf of Genoa, operating from th former German base at Leghorn an hunting down enemy convoys movin between Genoa and Spezia. Man lighters, merchant ships and barge were sunk, then as operations decline as the Germans retreated from Italy most of the PTs were withdrawn. Onl Squadron 22 remained, carrying ou patrols from Leghorn until the las days of the war.

By now, Allied maritime power ha been restored over most of the Mediter ranean. Apart from a short stretch o

astline in north west Italy, only the orthern Adriatic still remained in nemy hands, into whose waters the epleted S-boat flotillas had with-rawn, now formed into the 1st ivision under *Kapitänleutnant* uppermann. They concentrated their forts on minelaying operations in ne swept channels, to which a number MTBs and MLs fell victim during ne winter of 1944/45.

The Adriatic now became the centre Coastal Forces activity. The 20th, th and 57th flotillas were joined by ne 60th Flotilla from the Aegean and new 28th Flotilla of Vosper MTBs nder Lieutenant Charles Jerram SC, RNVR. Operating from bases nat steadily moved northward up the ast coast of Italy and, on the other de of the Adriatic, up the Dalmatian lands, the main task of the boats was cut off the German withdrawal. any craft were intercepted and nk – on one operation led by Jerram, three MTBs fired six torpedoes which sank five F-lighters, perhaps the highest success ratio of any torpedo attack.

The last successful action by Coastal Forces was on the night of 13th April, when two of Bligh's D-boats torpedoed and sank the ex-Italian torpedo-boat TA 45 off the Dalmatian coast. Unfortunately, three nights later, one of the D-boats struck a mine in an area which was supposed to have been cleared by the partisans, breaking the boat in half and killing most of her crew.

The end came on the evening of 4th May, two days after the surrender of all the German forces in Italy. In order not to fall into the hands of the partisans, Wuppermann loaded all the available diesel fuel into five of his S-boats and with 300 men in each of them, his entire force, he set out from Trieste to the Royal Navy's base at Ancona to surrender to a very surprised port commander.

A captured German F-lighter

The great invasion

While activities had been building up in the Mediterranean during 1943 and the first six months of 1944, Coastal Forces in Britain continued to maintain their guard over coastal convoys and had taken the fight against enemy shipping into an area that now extended from the Channel Islands to the Norwegian fjords. Towards the end of this period they began to prepare for their biggest single operation of the war – the D-Day landings in Normandy in June 1944, made by the greatest invasion armada the world had ever seen in which British MTBs, MGBs and MLs and American PT boats all took part. By then, Coastal Forces comprised no less than twenty-eight flotillas of MTBs/MGBs, twenty flotillas of MLs, and eleven of HDMLs. Four American PT squadrons were brought over from the Pacific to take part in the invasion, under the overall command of Lieutenant-Commander John Bulkeley.

This was the culmination of eighteen months of fierce activity in the narrow seas in which, from the beginning of 1943, the emphasis in Coastal Forces was on attack rather than defence. It now became a major undertaking for the S-boats to make sorties into the North Sea to lay mines or attack British convoys.

Flotilla of Vosper MTBs

Above: Concrete bunkers sheltered German S-boats at their Channel bases. *Right:* MGBs guarding the Allied supply lines off Normandy

When they did, it was usually in large numbers, dispersed over a wide area, in the hope that some might be able to slip through the offshore patrol screen.

For most of the time, the S-boats were required for escort duties with their own convoys, putting them in much the same defensive position as the MTBs during the first three years of the war. But the heavily escorted German convoys were more difficult targets to attack than the large, lightly escorted British convoys. Together with the fact that enemy shipping, particularly in the Dover Straits, was greatly reduced, there was an inevitable falling-off in the number of MTB actions in 1943.

This would have been much greater but for two factors; the better boats coming into service, including 'D'-type Fairmiles and improved Vosper and BPB craft, and a higher degree of sophistication in the techniques of night-fighting in small boats. Much of the credit for this was due to the establishment in mid-1942 of a training base at Weymouth (*HMS Bee*), where crews were instructed in gunnery, signals, torpedo drill and general tactics by some of the most successful commanders whose exploits had already become legend.

There had also developed a much greater degree of co-operation with other services concerned in coastal warfare, particularly Fighter Command and Coastal Command's Strike Wing, in which short-range aircraft worked with destroyers and MTBs from Nore and Dover Commands in operations against enemy convoys.

The decision was taken in the summer of 1943 to equip all the 'D'-type Fairmiles and most of the newer MGBs with torpedoes. For just as the early MTBs had found themselves often hampered by a lack of guns, a situation that had led to the development of MGBs, now the gunboats sometimes found themselves in an ideal position to make torpedo attacks but with no torpedoes to fire while the MTBs they were escorting were unable to get into satisfactory firing positions.

As the boats were converted, they rapidly proved the value of this combination by increasing the number of successful attacks on enemy convoys off the coast of Western Europe, especially as these were now being escorted by S-boats so that one craft often had to fight a gun battle as well as make a torpedo attack. The D-boats in particular, with their longer range and greater seaworthiness, were able to take the fight further afield and hunt in areas where least expected. Boats based in Yarmouth and the Shetlands were especially successful, regularly making long journeys across the North Sea.

But it was on the men who fought in small boats rather than the equipment

that the final results depended. There was still a place for the smaller MTBs when properly handled by such commanders as Peter Dickens. Together with the 11th MTB Flotilla under Lieutenant I C Trelawny DSC, RNVR, also based at Felixstowe, Dickens' 21st Flotilla specialised in the tactics of stalking and the unobserved approach, achieving some of the most successful results of the year.

In one operation early in the morning of 14th May, three MTBs led by Dickens sank two large minesweepers and damaged an S-boat off the Hook of Holland with only superficial damage to themselves. Later in the year, Dickens was given command of a Hunt-class destroyer, but the tactics that had become his hallmark were ably continued by other flotillas at Felixstowe.

Because of shore-based radar and regular MGB patrols, the S-boats were rarely able to penetrate the east coast shipping routes. But towards the end of the year, they tried to counter this defence with a series of well planned mass attacks in which as many as thirty S-boats sometimes took part. Such an attack by three S-boat flotillas took place on the night of 24th October against a northbound convoy off the Norfolk coast. It developed into a major battle, spread out over many hours and over a large area of the North Sea, with no less than sixteen separate encounters between German boats and British destroyers and coastal craft.

Although one British trawler, the *William Stephen,* was sunk after straggling some miles behind the convoy, the S-boats were driven off before they could make contact with the main body of the convoy. In addition, at least four of them were sunk – one after being rammed by MGB 607 (Lieutenant R M Marshall RNVR) – and a number of others damaged.

One reason for the more aggressive spirit shown by the German boats at this time was that they were now more heavily armed. It had been a long-standing complaint by their crews that although they were faster than the British boats, they suffered from inferior armament. During the winter of 1943/44 many of them were re-armed with 40mm guns in place of their previous 20mm guns, and from then on showed less reluctance to engage in a direct confrontation with the MTBs.

During four years of fighting by Coastal Forces, the North Sea had been the main arena. But in 1944 there was a switch to the English Channel as preparations were made for the biggest operation of them all, the landings in Normandy. A Captain of Coastal Forces, Channel, (Captain P V McLaughlin RN) was appointed to the staff of the Commander-in-Chief Portsmouth to take charge of MTB and ML support for the invasion. (MGBs were no longer to be designated separately.)

In April, American PT boats made their first appearance in British waters, brought over in the first place at the urgent request of the Office of Strategic Services to land and pick up agents on the French coast. These tasks were undertaken by Squadron 2, which had been re-commissioned after the Solomons campaign, and continued until the end of the year. Three other squadrons, numbers 30, 34 and 35, were also brought over to help in the actual invasion.

The primary task of the British and American boats was to help defend the flanks of the spearhead attack on the Normandy beaches and maintain guard over the subsequent flow of cross-Channel traffic. The most likely counter attacks were expected to come from destroyers, torpedo-boats, S-boats and minesweepers, which the Germans still had in large numbers based in the Low Countries and on the Atlantic coast of France.

In the weeks before the invasion, ten flotillas of MTBs and MLs were engaged on special missions to lay mines off the French coast, while at the same time other MTBs kept up their usual anti-S-boat patrols and the

MLs prepared for their wide range of tasks which were to include mine-sweeping, duties as escorts and navigational leaders, and shepherding in the landing craft.

Meanwhile, knowing an invasion was imminent although not when and where, the Germans were carrying out their own counter-measures. Large numbers of S-boats were out every night, laying mines and doing all they could to hamper the Allied preparations. Their biggest success came early in the morning of 28th April when nine of the Cherbourg-based S-boats attacked a convoy of American landing craft in Lyme Bay which were taking part in an invasion rehearsal. Two were sunk and another damaged, with a heavy loss of life – there were over 600 military and naval casualties.

Of the total of 1,213 warships that gathered along the south coast early in June to take part in the invasion – in addition to more than 4,000 landing craft of various types – 495 were coastal craft, including MTBs, PTs, SGBs,

Return from night patrol

MLs and HDMLs. Most of the PTs were allocated to the Western Task Force, together with the SGBs. A further 292 coastal craft under the Home Commands were also to help in the initial phase of the invasion; they included Dutch, French and Norwegian-crewed boats.

This mighty armada set sail in the early hours of 6th June towards Normandy. They were half-way across the Channel when the news was flashed to the S-boat flotillas at Boulogne, Cherbourg and Le Havre, together with orders to put to sea immediately. But as the heavy doors of the bunkers which sheltered the flotillas opened and the boats nosed their way into the harbours, the first waves of British and American bombers appeared out of low cloud to bomb the coastal installations. It would have been suicide for the boats to remain at sea under such a bombardment. The Boulogne and Le Havre flotillas were forced to return to their bunkers. Only those from Cherbourg managed to approach anywhere near the invasion fleet but they were beaten back by the destroyers and MTBs guarding the flanks. They too were compelled to return to base.

The only enemy action at sea against the landings that morning was by three *Möwe* class torpedo-boats which managed to penetrate the exposed flank of one of the invasion forces and sank the Norwegian destroyer *Svenner*. But then these boats too had to turn back from the overwhelming forces ranged against them, luckily escaping in a smokescreen which the British themselves had just laid as a defence against air attack.

The landings were more successful than anyone had dared hope, taking the Germans completely by surprise. The Luftwaffe was entirely absent, and those coastal defences which survived the Allied bombing and naval bombardment along the fifty mile front were demoralised by the sheer weight of the assault. By the end of the day all the beaches had been taken and the leading troops were already pushing inland while fresh waves of men and supplies were landed.

The initial element of surprise could not last for long, of course. As the Germans recovered, they began to counter attack the cross-Channel supply route to the Allied forces. S-boats from Cherbourg and Le Havre, the ports on either side of the Allied bridgehead, were out on the first night after the invasion. And so began a series of clashes with MTBs that were to rage nightly in the narrow seas until September, when German shipping was finally driven out of the Channel into the North Sea.

It was primarily against the eastern flank of the British area that the attack was concentrated, because Le Havre was the most heavily defended port and where most of the German destroyers and smaller craft were based. Losses among the Cherbourg-based S-boats were so high during the first week of the invasion that those remaining were also tranferred to Le Havre. Thus the PTs in the western area had no contact at all with S-boats from the time of the invasion until August when they were withdrawn from Normandy, some to operate in the vicinity of the Channel Islands while others were attached to Portsmouth to work with British MTBs patrolling the eastern flank.

It had been largely due to the efforts of these craft that supply ships in the eastern area were kept virtually free from surface attack. Of the host of Allied shipping in Seine Bay, only two LSTs and six smaller landing craft were sunk during the first week of the invasion. German losses caused by Coastal Forces were three S-boats and one R-boat as against two MTBs sunk.

The greatest disaster to the S-boats came on 14th June when Lancasters of Bomber Command raided the bunkers at Le Havre and destroyed eleven S-boats, three torpedo-boats and many

smaller vessels in the harbour. The 6th S-boat Flotilla was moved down from Boulogne at the end of the month to help make up the losses, but it was some weeks before the Germans were able to resume their patrols.

The German evacuation from Cherbourg at the end of June gave the MTBs a chance to renew their attack after so many days of defensive patrols. Two groups of boats of the 14th MTB Flotillas destroyed all but one of the last enemy convoy to leave the harbour, and that was later sunk by gunfire from other MTBs.

In spite of the odds against them, the S-boats fought on tenaciously. Patrols from Le Havre clashed constantly with frigates and MTBs with the losses about even for both sides. But none managed to get through to attack the invasion supply routes. In an effort to hamper this traffic, the Germans turned to the use of human torpedoes and motor boats loaded with explosives, which the operator aimed at a target and then jumped

clear at the last minute to be picked up by another boat. But such methods were rarely successful. The MTBs and MLs usually managed to destroy them before they could get anywhere near the Allied ships.

With the MTBs and other ships making it almost impossible to approach the cross-Channel convoys, the S-boats turned their attention to the less heavily protected south coast convoys. They made a number of successful forays, including the sinking of five merchant ships off Beachy Head at the end of July. And the mines they laid posed a serious threat.

In the western area meanwhile, MTBs and PTs operating from Plymouth and Dartmouth were gradually clearing enemy shipping from the Channel Islands and the Brittany coast. Combined with the invasion of southern France, this area ceased to be of any military importance by the end of August. Enemy

The steam gunboat _Grey Goose_

A German S-boat surrenders at the end of the war

garrisons were cut off and either surrendered immediately or were left powerless and inactive until the end of the war.

Off the Normandy coast on the other hand, the battles were becoming more intensive as the Germans tried to break through the Allied blockade of Le Havre to bring in supplies and reinforcements. In nightly battles with MTBs and destroyers, those S-boats still operational were gradually whittled down to less than a dozen. Eventually, at the end of August, the Germans had to evacuate Le Havre with what was left of their

shipping. As they sailed north-eastwards up the Channel, slipping in by day into the harbours of Fécamp, Dieppe and Boulogne for protection, they were hounded all the way by MTBs, reducing their numbers still further. By 1st September, all German shipping had been driven through the Dover Straits into the temporary shelter of Belgian and Dutch ports. The English Channel was cleared of the enemy for the first time in over four years. During the three months from D-Day, MTBs alone sank thirty-four enemy craft and nine possibles, for the loss of ten boats themselves, three in action with S-boats and the others by mines. The S-boats sank eleven craft and damaged eight others, but

form of attack by S-boats. In the first three months of 1945, these caused the sinking of twenty-six Allied merchant ships off the east coast of Britain, for the loss of only four S-boats. The MTBs were constantly out on patrol, but while they invariably managed to drive off a direct S-boat attack, they could not always prevent the fast German boats from slipping through the offshore screen when on mine-laying operations.

Although the final outcome of the war was by now inevitable, the S-boats were determined to fight until the very last moment. It was only in April that they were finally beaten in a series of fierce encounters with MTBs that to a large extent were only made possible by the very effective airborne radar developed by the RAF. Air patrols could now detect enemy craft almost as soon as they left harbour and track them all the way across the North Sea until the MTBs could be vectored to their position. In such circumstances the S-boats had very little chance. After a group had been intercepted in the Scheldt Estuary on the night of 12th April and driven off with severe damage, they returned to base and there they remained until the end of the war. The only other occasion when the S-boats put to sea was on 13th May, after Germany's unconditional surrender, when two of them flying the white flag sailed from Rotterdam to Felixstowe, bringing members of the German naval staff who were to inform Nore Command of the location of enemy minefields.

The two boats were escorted into harbour by ten MTBs, on board which were most of the Senior Officers of the east coast flotillas. After so many nights of fighting against each other, as well as coping with common hardships in the gale-blown North Sea, the crews of the opposing sides met face to face for the first time, while the British could make their first detailed examination of the elusive *Schnellboote* which had been a menace to shipping for so long.

from all causes lost fifty-three boats themselves.

During all this time there had been a lull in fighting in the North Sea. Now activity in this area increased sharply as British and German boats returned from the English Channel. Successful actions were fought by both sides, but as the Allied forces on land gradually drove the Germans from their coastal bases, the scope of S-boat activity was increasingly limited. It would have been even less but for the mistaken decision by the Allies not to take Antwerp immediately, leaving the River Scheldt open to the Germans.

As throughout the war, the laying of mines was still the most effective

Across the Pacific

The US Navy's victory at the Battle of Midway in June 1942 not only stemmed the tide of Japanese conquests eastwards across the Pacific but enabled American forces to turn from the defensive to the attack. Their first great offensive action of the Pacific war took place on 7th August with the US Marine landings on Guadalcanal, heralding the beginning of the Solomons campaign by the South Pacific Force.

It was soon apparent that PT boats would be extremely useful in the kind of warfare taking place among the Solomon Islands. A new Squadron 3

was formed, under the command of Lieutenant-Commander Alan Montgomery USN, and the first eight boats were shipped to Tulagi on 12th October. Two nights later they were in action for the first time when the Japanese, determined to regain control of the southern Solomons, sent a heavy task force to shell US installations on Guadalcanal in preparation for a major landing on the island.

As soon as the Japanese ships began their bombardment, Montgomery took four of the PTs from Tulagi into the attack against them. One of the boats, PT 38 commanded by Lieutenant (jg)

Robert Searles USNR, after becoming separated from the others, managed to score torpedo hits against a light cruiser. PT 60, commanded by Searles' brother, Lieutenant (jg) John Searles USNR with Montgomery on board, also hit a destroyer but later ran aground on a coral reef.

This action, the first by PTs since the withdrawal from the Philippines, was typical of many during the following months as the enemy threw ever-increasing numbers of cruisers

Zebra stripe camouflage to confuse the enemy

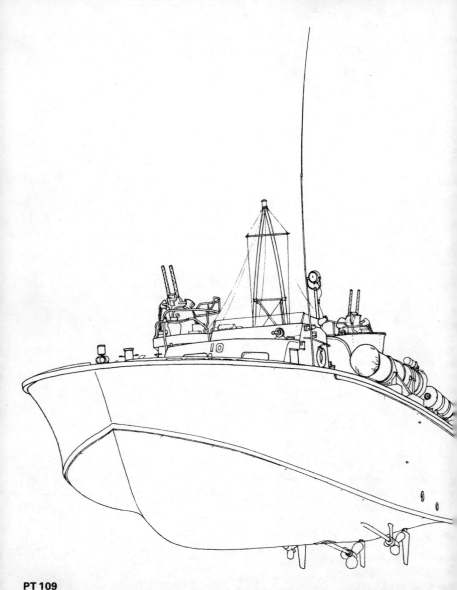

PT 109
The Elco-type boat commanded by the late John F Kennedy. *Dimensions:* 80 feet by 20¾ feet. *Crew:* 14 *Engines:* Three Packard petrol motors, 4,050bhp. *Speed:* 40 knots. *Armament:* Four 21-inch torpedo tubes, two 20mm anti-aircraft guns

nd destroyers in an effort to drive the Americans from Guadalcanal. For both sides it had become a race to land and supply sufficiently large forces to be able to hold the island. The Japanese shuttle-service of reinforcements was known as the 'Tokyo Express' and it was against these convoys that the PTs directed their main efforts. Night after night the boats of Squadron, later supported by the arrival of Squadron 2 from Panama, lay in wait in the shallow coastal waters to harass the enemy and to act as scouts for the larger American warships.

The battle for Guadalcanal lasted six months, until in February 1943 the Japanese admitted defeat and withdrew their troops from the island. During that time the PTs sank at least four destroyers and many smaller vessels, as well as much of the equipment that the Japanese tried to boat ashore, and damaged a number of other ships. So effective were they that often their presence alone in offshore waters at night was sufficient to persuade enemy supply convoys to turn back.

With Guadalcanal finally in American hands, the way was now open to the upper Solomon islands, into which the Japanese had withdrawn and were concentrating on building up their defences. The next big offensive came in June with American landings on the New Georgia group of islands, 200 miles north west of Guadalcanal. By then four more PT squadrons had arrived, including Squadron 9 commanded by Lieutenant-Commander Robert Kelly who had earlier served in the Philippines, and more were on their way. The squadrons were combined into Motor Torpedo Boat Flotilla 1, under Commander Allen Calvert USN, while for administration and logistics support, Captain M M Dupre Jr USN was appointed Commander Motor Torpedo Boat Squadrons, South Pacific (Administrative). New PT bases were established, of which the largest was at Rendova Harbour on Lumbari Island. It was from here, during the night of 1st August, that the PTs took part in a major encounter with the Tokyo Express. Four Japanese destroyers were heading through Blackett Strait in an attempt to reach the Japanese base on the southern point of Kolombangara Island. Knowing that the only US forces in a position to oppose them were the Rendova-based PTs, the Japanese carried out an air attack on the base earlier in the day, during which two boats were destroyed and several others damaged. When the time came however, it was still possible to send out fifteen PTs to intercept the four destroyers.

The engagement that followed was a disappointing failure, mainly because the newly arrived squadrons had not yet learned the value of working together. The boats attacked independently, neglecting to inform others when they located the enemy with the result that half the force found no targets at all. The uncoordinated attacks made by the rest were easily beaten off and none of the thirty torpedoes fired could be confirmed as hits. The only notable event was the ramming of one of the PTs by the destroyer *Amagiri*, which caused the loss of the boat and damage to the destroyer. In command of the boat, PT 109, was Lieutenant John F Kennedy USNR – seventeen years later to become President of the United States.

The impact of the crash, which occurred as Kennedy was turning to starboard in an attempt to fire torpedoes at the destroyer, broke the boat in half. Two of the crew were killed instantly, and as a fire had broken out from gasoline spilling onto the surface of the water, Kennedy ordered the survivors to abandon ship. Luckily the wake created by the departing destroyer carried off the burning gasoline and the crew managed to swim back to that part of the boat that was still afloat. Kennedy himself rescued three of the men who were suffering from burns.

The broken hull of PT 109 drifted helplessly all night. As the sun came up the following morning it was obvious to the eleven survivors on board that she would soon sink. They were about four miles northeast of Gizo, within sight of a number of small islands but uncertain which of them might be occupied by the Japanese. Kennedy had to make the decision to abandon the sinking boat and try to swim to one of these islands. He himself towed the most badly burned member of the crew; the others towed two non-swimmers on a boat rigged from part of the gun mounting.

After several hours in the water, all the survivors managed to reach the island. Later that evening, Kennedy decided to swim into Ferguson Passage in an attempt to intercept any of the PT boats that might be patrolling the area. That night however they were operating off Gizo and not in Blackett Strait as usual. Kennedy had to return to the island without sighting any friendly boats. He was just swimming the final lap when he was caught in a current which swept him back about two miles to where he had started and had to make the return trip all over again. He was completely exhausted and feverish when he eventually arrived back on the island just after dawn and slept for most of the day.

The following night Ensign Ross made a similar attempt to intercept PT patrols from Rendova but was also unsuccessful. Up to this time all that the group had to live on were coconuts, but now even these were running short, and so at noon on 4th August, using the same towing arrangements as before, they swam to another small island. Luckily this also was not occupied by the Japanese, but it had an equally limited supply of coconuts. The next morning, Kennedy and Ross swam to a larger neighbouring island in search of anything that might be useful to the group. They found a

canoe and supplies of food and water left by the Japanese.

That night Kennedy again made the journey into Ferguson Passage, this time by canoe, but still no PTs were sighted. On his return to the island he found that the group had met two natives who had paddled ashore by canoe. After the Americans had managed to convince them that they were not Japanese, the natives helped in every way possible. A message was sent to the nearest American base and eventually on 8th August, after being marooned for seven days, Kennedy and his crew were rescued by a PT boat from Rendova.

The action in which PT 109 had been involved was the last major encounter with destroyers of the Tokyo Express.

Soon after the New Georgia landings the Japanese had lost so many of their larger warships because of the dominance of American seapower that they turned instead to the use of coastal barges for transporting troops and keeping their island bases supplied.

These barges, which could operate in waters too shallow for the larger American ships, were able to hide close in shore by day to escape attack by aircraft and became the principal quarry for the PTs. They were by no means an easy target. As well as being well armoured so that gunfire was often ineffective against them, the Japanese countered the attacks by PTs by mounting heavier guns, up to 40mm. They also installed shore batteries along the barge routes. The Americans in their turn re-equipped some of the PTs with 37mm and 40mm guns, making up for the increased weight by removing torpedo tubes and depth charges so that they came to fight as motor gunboats.

Although the opposing craft were similarly armed, the PTs had the supremacy of speed which from the beginning enabled them to establish a clear ascendancy over the barges. By the end of the year the PTs had sunk about forty barges and seriously damaged many more.

T off the coast of Attu

In addition to hampering Japanese efforts to reinforce their island bases, the PTs were also used to transport troops and marines in taking over the smaller islands and for carrying out reconnaissance missions prior to major landings. By now American strategy was not to occupy all the islands but to move forward in a by-passing technique which was to leave tens of thousands of Japanese cut off from their supplies and even from retreat. As the American forces advanced across the Solomons, so the PTs moved up with them, operating from new forward bases at Lever on the northeast coast of New Georgia, at Lambu Lambu on the island of Vella Lavella, and on Purnata Island following the landings by US Marines on Bougainville, largest of the Solomon islands.

The ultimate objective of the campaign was the Japanese stronghold at Rabaul, on the northeastern point of New Britain. This had been occupied by the enemy within three weeks of the fall of Manila and used as a base from which to advance on two fronts, one force extending southeastwards across the Solomons and the other extending southwestwards into New Guinea with the object of isolating Australia before launching an invasion.

During the summer of 1942 the Japanese advanced rapidly down the north coast of Papua and across the island towards Port Moresby, the last Allied base north of Australia itself. Here they were stopped in September in a desperate fight with Australian troops. With the arrival soon afterwards of American units of the Southwest Pacific Force, began the arduous task of driving the Japanese back through the swamps and jungles of eastern New Guinea. In this campaign also the PTs played a vital role.

The first boats arrived at Milne Bay, on the eastern point of Papua, in December 1942. There were only six to begin with, commanded by Lieutenant Daniel Baughman USN, but in their first action on the night of Christmas Eve they not only torpedoed and sank the Japanese submarine I-22 but also destroyed two troop-carrying barges in Douglas Harbour. This was the first of many successful actions against enemy barges in New Guinea, just as similar actions were taking place in the Solomons.

By March 1943, further PT squadrons had arrived at Milne Bay, including Squadron 7 under Lieutenant-Commander John Bulkeley. The PTs were designated as Task Group 70.1 (Motor Torpedo Boat Squadrons Seventh Fleet) under the overall command of Commander Morton C Mumma Jr USN. He was responsible directly to the Fleet Commander which did much to simplify PT operations.

The PTs operated at this time from a main base at Kana Kopa. But they faced formidable problems. Owing to the difficulty of transportation in a country of swamp and jungle with one of the highest rainfalls in the world there was an extreme shortage of supplies and spare parts. For months in order to maintain patrols, generators had to be transferred from boats returning from duty to others going out as there were just not enough to go round. Nevertheless, the PTs were able to play their part in the total destruction of a large Japanese convoy in the Bismarck Sea early in March.

The convoy consisted of eight destroyers and eight merchant ships carrying 7,000 troops and supplies to reinforce the enemy positions at Lae and Salamana. Their arrival would have meant a serious threat to the lightly held Allied positions along the coast. Waves of American and Australian aircraft made concerted attacks on the convoy, to such effect that by the night of the 3rd only one destroyer and one large merchant ship were still afloat, both in a damaged condition. It was at this point that they came within range of PTs from an advance base at Tufi, led by the commander of Squadron 8, Lieutenant-Commander Barry K Atkins USN. The

's sank the merchant ship, the *~awa Maru* (6,493 tons), and further ~maged the destroyer which was ~ally sunk by aircraft the following ~y.

~his setback to the enemy was due ~marily to Allied superiority in the ~ and the fact that the Japanese ~re already so heavily committed in ~ Solomons. It proved to the Japanese ~t they could no longer transport ~plies from Rabaul to New Guinea ~ escorted convoys. Instead they had ~ fall back on the use of coastal ~ges, moving by night, and as in the ~lomons these became the major ~get for the PTs.

~ithin a period of two months, the ~s from Tufi sank eighteen barges. ~ the Allied forces advanced slowly ~ the coast of New Guinea, the PTs ~ved with them, establishing for-~rd bases at Douglas Harbour and ~robe from where they could patrol ~ Huon Gulf. At the end of June they ~ved for the first time as troop

PT under way. Note radar dome and torpedoes in side-launching racks

carriers during the landings at Nassau Bay, an operation planned in co-ordination with the New Georgia landings by the South Pacific Force.

Towards the end of 1943 the older boats were replaced as new squadrons, notably the 12th and 21st, took over. Now began one of the fiercest battles of the campaign as the Japanese made a determined stand in the Huon Peninsula and tried to reinforce their positions with bargeloads of troops and supplies from New Britain and from bases further up the New Guinea coast. The number of PT actions greatly increased, with the boats often sailing one hundred miles or more to reach the enemy's coastal shipping routes. By the end of November over one hundred more barges had been sunk and others damaged. But some of the PTs had also been lost, mainly by grounding on uncharted reefs as they worked close inshore to intercept barges that were trying to slip undetected down the coast.

Barge-hunting was a hazardous operation, a fact reflected in the Presidential Unit Citation awarded to Motor Torpedo Boat Squadrons 12 and 21 – one of only two such citations made to PTs. (The other was to Squadron 3 for its work in the Solomon Islands.)

'For outstanding performance during the Huon Peninsula Campaign against enemy Japanese forces from October 1943 to March 1944. Highly vulnerable to damage from treacherous reefs and grounding during close inshore patrols, MTB Squadrons 12 and 21 spearheaded a determined waterborne attack on the enemy, boldly penetrating hostile waters and disrupting barge traffic vital to the maintenance of Japanese strongholds in the New Guinea area. Dauntlessly exchanging gunfire with heavily armoured gunboats and barges, airplanes and shore emplacements, the boats of Squadrons 12 and 21 have successfully diverted hostile artillery fire to themselves in protection of Allied land forces; they have steadily destroyed the enemy's ships carrying troops, food and combat supplies; they have captured Japanese personnel, landed in hostile territory, and effected air and sea rescue missions. Tenacious and indomitable in the face of superior fire-power and despite frequent damage to boats and casualties among personnel, the officers and men of Squadrons 12 and 21 have fought gallantly and served with distinction in crushing enemy resistance in the strategically important area.'

The commanders of these two squadrons, which were made up of eighty-foot Elcos, were Lieutenant-Commander John Harllee USN (12), and Commander Selman Bowling USN (21).

At the end of November an advance was established at Dreger Harbour which eventually took over from Kana Kopa as the main PT supply a[nd] repair centre in New Guinea. T[he] following two months saw landings [by] the US Army at Arawe on the sout[h] west coast of New Britain and [at] Saidor on the New Guinea coa[st] again extending the distances that t[he] PT patrols had to cover. Early in 19[44] Squadrons 12 and 21 at Dreger we[re] joined by a number of boats fro[m] Squadrons 7 and 8 and three n[ew] squadrons – 18 (Lieutenant M S Sw[ift] USNR), 24 (Lieutenant-Commander Burt Davis Jr USN), and 25 (Lie[u]tenant-Commander James Thomps[on] USNR). As a result of their activit[ies] up until the end of February 1944, wh[en] the Japanese were forced to withdr[aw] from the Huon Peninsula, some 1[ ] barges had been sunk or destroye[d] During February, Commander Bowli[ng] took over as Commander Mot[or] Torpedo Boat Squadrons Seven[th] Fleet and his command of Squadron [21] fell to Lieutenant Paul Rennell USN[.]

The New Guinea PTs were n[ow] carrying out patrols as far east as t[he] dividing line between the Southwe[st] Pacific and South Pacific Forces [at] Cape Lambert, only forty miles fr[om] Rabaul. Their operations covered fo[ur] distinct areas – the New Guinea coa[st,] the Admiralty Islands, and northe[rn] and southern New Britain. The n[et] was gradually being drawn tigh[t] around the Japanese stronghold [of] Rabaul as the two great Allied For[ces] fought their way closer to each oth[er.] In mid-February, realising that t[he] situation was hopeless, the Japane[se] evacuated most of their air streng[th] from New Britain. But the 40,0[00] Japanese troops at Rabaul were l[ess] fortunate. With the occupation of t[he] Admiralties by the Southwest Paci[fic] Force and of Emirau Island by t[he] South Pacific Force, they were caug[ht] in a trap from which there was [no] escape. On 1st March, the first All[ied] vessel since the Japanese occupati[on] entered Rabaul Harbour – PT 319, o[ne] of a force of twelve boats from Gre[en] Island led by Commander Spec[ ] which had taken part in a joint atta[ck]

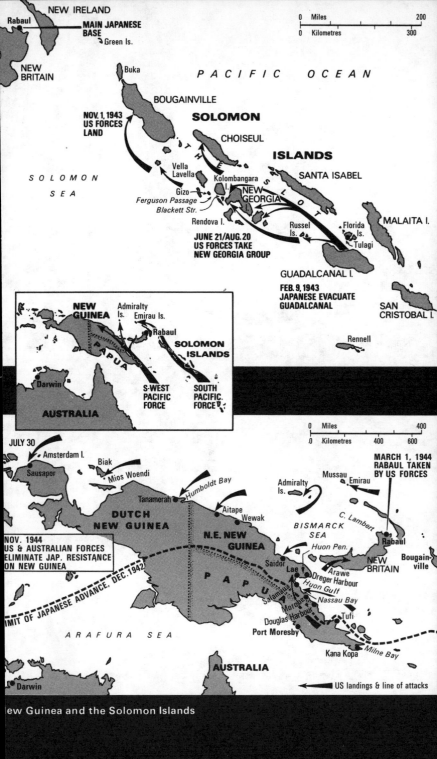

NEW IRELAND

Rabaul

MAIN JAPANESE BASE

Green Is.

NEW BRITAIN

Buka

PACIFIC OCEAN

BOUGAINVILLE

SOLOMON

NOV. 1, 1943 US FORCES LAND

CHOISEUL

ISLANDS

SANTA ISABEL

SOLOMON SEA

Vella Lavella

Kolombangara I.

NEW GEORGIA

Gizo

Ferguson Passage
Blackett Str.

Rendova I.

Russel Is.

Florida Is.

MALAITA I.

Tulagi

JUNE 21/AUG. 20 US FORCES TAKE NEW GEORGIA GROUP

GUADALCANAL I.

FEB. 9, 1943 JAPANESE EVACUATE GUADALCANAL

SAN CRISTOBAL I.

Rennell

NEW GUINEA

Admiralty Is.

Emirau Is.

Rabaul

SOLOMON ISLANDS

PAPUA

Darwin

S-WEST PACIFIC FORCE

SOUTH PACIFIC FORCE

AUSTRALIA

JULY 30

Amsterdam I.

Sausapor

Biak

Mios Woendi

Tanamerah

Humboldt Bay

DUTCH NEW GUINEA

Aitape

Wewak

Mussau

Emirau

MARCH 1, 1944 RABAUL TAKEN BY US FORCES

Admiralty Is.

C. Lambert

N.E. NEW GUINEA

BISMARCK SEA

Huon Pen.

Rabaul

NEW BRITAIN

Bougain-ville

NOV. 1944 US & AUSTRALIAN FORCES ELIMINATE JAP. RESISTANCE ON NEW GUINEA

Saidor

Lae

Arawe

Dreger Harbour

Huon Gulf

P A P U A

Salamaua

Morobe

Nassau Bay

Tufi

LIMIT OF JAPANESE ADVANCE, DEC. 1942

Douglas Harbour

Port Moresby

ARAFURA SEA

Kana Kopa

Milne Bay

AUSTRALIA

Darwin

US landings & line of attacks

ew Guinea and the Solomon Islands

ith destroyers.

With the fall of Rabaul, the ultimate bjective of the South Pacific campaign as achieved. It now became the task f the PTs operating in the Solomons o prevent the escape of Japanese roops isolated in their island garisons. Many more enemy barges were ntercepted and sunk during these perations, which lasted until the end f the year, under the overall command f Commodore Edward. Moran USN. Ieanwhile, a number of the PT quadrons were transferred to New uinea where heavy fighting was still aking place.

At the end of April, the Southwest acific Force launched the biggest of s by-passing operations with simulneous landings at Humboldt and anahonerah, 400 miles northwest of reger Harbour, and at Aitape nother hundred miles further up ne coast. The 50,000 troops of the 18th nperial Japanese Army who thus ecame isolated between Wewak and ansa countered by moving westards against Aitape. Again, because f the impenetrable jungle inland, ney had to depend heavily on barges s the only means of maintaining their pply lines. And again the PTs were rought in to deal with this traffic. quadrons 7 and 8 were moved to itape and Squadrons 12 and 18 to umboldt Bay.

The main activity took place off itape. During the five months they ere based there, the PTs sank or estroyed over one hundred barges and lso damaged many Japanese coastal nstallations. The PTs suffered little amage themselves; eleven were hit y enemy fire but only one, PT 133, was estroyed. Casualties were also markably light – three men killed nd seven wounded. The same could ot be said of the troop-laden enemy arges. The great majority of the

Japanese, after their barges had been sunk, resisted capture and preferred deliberately to drown themselves rather than be taken on board the PTs.

By early June, as the American and Australian forces pressed further into northwest New Guinea with landings on the islands of Wakde and Biak, the PT repair and supply base at Dreger had to be moved forward to Mios Woendi, a small coral atoll ten miles south of Biak. With its deep water lagoon and flat, sandy beach, sheltered by palm trees, it was the most ideal base that the PTs found in New Guinea. But by now the enemy's coastal traffic was dwindling. Unable to find a means of dealing effectively with the PTs and having lost so many hundreds of barges, the Japanese, who were systematically withdrawing from the areas they had once conquered with such ease, preferred to carry out their evacuation overland. This meant a hazardous trek through swamp and jungle, harassment during the day by air attack, and the abandonment of most of their equipment. But it was better than almost certain failure at the hands of the PTs.

The last PT base to be established in New Guinea was on Amsterdam Island, 250 miles west of Mios Woendi, following the landing at Cape Sansapor on 30th July which gave the Allies final domination of the north coast. Patrols from here and Mios Woendi were carried out until mid-November by squadrons which included the first Higgins boats to arrive in the Southwest Pacific. But although a further number of barges were sunk, the peak of the fighting in this area was now over.

Even before the Japanese had completed the evacuation of their depleted forces from New Guinea, the Americans were taking the first steps towards the final great campaign of the Pacific war – the liberation of the Philippines. PTs from the Solomons and New Guinea were again in the van of the attack.

olding field-glasses, Commander S Bowling (commanding Motor rpedo Squadrons Seventh Fleet) serves operations off Morotai

Before a major invasion of the Philippines by the US Sixth Army, commanded by Lieutenant-General Walter Krueger, could begin, it was necessary to establish an island base between the northern tip of New Guinea and Mindanao, the most southerly of the Philippine islands, from which air support could be provided. There were two possibilities – Halmahera and Morotai – both islands still in Japanese hands. The latter was chosen, and on 15th September 1944 a landing there

was made by the Morotai Task Force under Rear Admiral Daniel E Barbey

Halmahera was held in greater strength by the Japanese than Morotai, which was one reason for this choice. The two islands were separated by a stretch of water only twelve miles wide and it was vital to prevent the numerically superior Japanese forces on Halmahera from launching counter attack while the fight for Morotai was taking place. It was task assigned primarily to the PTs

Philippines

the day following the Morotai nding, Commander Bowling, who s now commanding the Motor rpedo Boat Squadrons of the venth Fleet, arrived with forty-one s and two tenders from Squadrons 10, 18 and 33, and patrols between the o islands commenced that same ght. They were continued without a eak until the end of the war eleven onths later. No less than fifty barges d 150 other small craft were interpted and destroyed by the PTs as the

Japanese attempted to reinforce their small garrison on Morotai. It was eventually found that 37,000 Japanese had been kept isolated on Halmahera during that time.

The first PT action in fact took place on the afternoon of 16th September when the crews of two boats, PTs 489 and 363, volunteered to go on a dangerous daylight mission to rescue the pilot of a US Navy carrier-borne

Approaching Corregidor

fighter who had been shot down while giving air support during the previous day's landing. He had drifted in a rubber raft to within 200 yards of an enemy-occupied beach at Wasile Bay on Halmahera. Other navy planes had circled the area to keep the pilot in sight and to strafe the Japanese gun positions, but all attempts by a Catalina flying-boat to rescue him had failed, owing to heavy anti-aircraft fire.

The two PTs were led by Lieutenant A Murray Preston USNR, commander of Squadron 33. For three hours, from the time of their arrival at Wasile Bay until they left after rescuing the pilot, they were under constant fire from Japanese shore batteries, and only managed to avoid being hit by zig-zagging at high speed across a mine-field. Miraculously no one was hurt and only minor damage was done to the boats. For this action, Lieutenant Preston was awarded the Medal of Honor, one of only two such awards made to PT men during the entire war. (The other was to Lieutenant Bulkeley for his exploits in the Philippines in 1942.)

With bases established on Morotai, General MacArthur's original plan was to begin the Philippines campaign by invading Mindanao. But by mid-September, carrier planes of Admiral Halsey's Third Fleet had been so successful in their operations against Japanese forces and installations in the area, destroying over 200 enemy aircraft, sinking many ships, and battering shore defences, that he suggested Mindanao could be by-passed and the landings made instead at Leyte, further to the north and intended to be the second objective once Mindanao was captured. This plan was agreed by Admiral Nimitz, Commander-in-Chief of US naval forces in the Pacific, and approved by MacArthur. And so the attack on Leyte took place on 20th October, two months earlier than originally planned.

Troops were landed by ships of the

Seventh Fleet, while Halsey's powerf Third Fleet provided naval and a support. As at Morotai, the P arrived as soon as the first landin had been made and started patro that night. There were forty-five boa to begin with from Squadrons 7, 12, 33 and 36, which had made the 1,20 mile voyage from Mios Woendi in Ne Guinea under their own power, refue ling from tenders. Commander Bowlin sailed with them. During the first thr nights on patrol off Leyte, they sa seven enemy barges and a freight But it was on the fourth night, 24 October, that they saw their fierce action during the Battle of Leyte Gu one of the great naval engagements the war.

Having suffered a serious breach their inner defences by the landings Leyte, the Japanese decided for t first time since Guadalcanal to ri an all-out naval engagement in

Right: PTs stand by during Japanese bombing attack in Leyte Gulf. *Below:* PT moves in to pick up survivors from bombed landing craft in Leyte Gulf

Left: **Japanese survivor is picked up after the Battle of Surigao Strait**
Above: **One of the many Japanese suicide boats shot up on the beach by PTs**

attempt to win back the initiative. Three great Japanese task forces were sent to converge on Leyte Gulf. The first was heading from the south through the Sulu Sea in the direction of Surigao Strait between Leyte and Mindanao. A second larger force was approaching San Bernardino Strait from the west. And an even more powerful carrier and battleship force was approaching Cape Engano from the north.

It was in the battle against the first of these enemy forces that the PTs took part. The force was divided into two groups; in the van, led by Vice-Admiral Shoji Nishimuta, were two battleships, a heavy cruiser and four destroyers, and about twenty miles behind, under the command of Vice-

Admiral Kiyohide Shima, came two heavy cruisers, a light cruiser, and a further four destroyers.

Opposing them was the US Seventh Fleet commanded by Rear-Admiral Jesse B Oldendorf. Comprising as it did six battleships, eight cruisers, twenty-five destroyers and thirty-nine PTs, the Americans under normal circumstances would have had much greater firepower than the Japanese. But most of their ammunition had been used up during the invasion bombardment. A long engagement would be disastrous. Every shell had to count, which meant that it was vital to have accurate information about the enemy's movements.

It was here that the PTs were to play an important role. As the enemy force steamed through the Mindanao Sea on the night of 24th October, the PTs were widely dispersed in sections of three to keep watch for their approach and to report back to the main American force which was strung out across the northern end of Surigao Strait, guarding the entrance to Leyte Gulf. In the Gulf was the enemy's main target – the transport shipping which had taken part in the invasion and which was still engaged in landing American troops and supplies.

Shortly before midnight, a section of PTs stationed in the Mindanao Sea picked up the leading Japanese ships by radar. The weather by this time had deteriorated, with low cloud and frequent rain squalls limiting visibility. Although it was only a secondary part of their mission to carry out an actual attack, the PTs at once moved towards the enemy. Before they could get within torpedo range, however, the big guns of the enemy opened fire on them at a distance of three miles. PT 152 (Lieutenant [jg] Joseph Eddin USN) was hit and set on fire and one of her gunners killed. As she and the other two boats retired behind smokescreens, pursued by a destroy and two cruisers while the Japane battleships continued to fire at lo range, the concussion caused bursting shells put all their radios o of action. It was not until contact w made with another PT section at te minutes past midnight that the fir report could be sent back to warn the approaching enemy force.

Meanwhile, more PTs were movi in to the attack. Although the scored many 40mm hits the heavi enemy firepower was so intense th most of the torpedoes fired miss their targets. One torpedo hit on destroyer was claimed by PT 4 (Lieutenant [jg] Richard Brown USN but shortly afterwards the boat w hit by 4.7-inch shells, killing two m and wounding Lieutenant Brown, h second officer and three men. The bo was beached and later sank.

As accurate reports of the positio course and speed of the enemy we received from the PTs, the ma American force prepared to spring i

PT Base 17 at Bobon Point, Samar

rap. First came a succession of three co-ordinated torpedo attacks by destroyers, then the battleships and cruisers opened fire with devastating accuracy. The two Japanese battleships and three destroyers were hit and disabled almost before they could open fire.

The heavy cruiser and the remaining destroyer turned and made a run for it back through the Surigao Strait. One of the boats patrolling the Strait PT 137 (Lieutenant [jg] Isadore Kovar USN), fired a torpedo at the fleeing destroyer at 03.35. The torpedo missed. But it was at this moment that the second Japanese force entered the Strait. The torpedo ploughed on through the water and struck the light cruiser *Abukuma*. She was so badly damaged, with her speed reduced to ten knots, that she had to drop out of formation. (She was later sunk by American bombers off Mindanao on the 26th, together with the heavy cruiser of the leading enemy force.)

This incident threw Admiral Shima's force off balance. When shortly afterwards he came across the burning wrecks of Admiral Nishimuta's force and realised the full extent of its destruction, he turned and fled, losing a destroyer on the way.

Lieutenant Kovar's action against the *Abukuma*, for which he was awarded the Navy Cross, was the most dramatic success of the PTs that night. But of even more importance had been their work in scouting and relaying back information on the enemy's movements, so that the American warships could attack with precision before running out of their limited supply of ammunition.

At the same time that the battle in Surigao Strait was taking place, Admiral Halsey's Third Fleet defeated the northern Japanese force off Cape Engano and Rear Admiral Sprague's escort carriers and destroyers managed to hold off the enemy force approaching from the west. In these actions and the aircraft attacks which followed, the Japanese lost four carriers, a battleship, six cruisers and four destroyers, and fifteen other ships were damaged. As Admiral Nimitz later reported: 'Our invasion of the Philippines was not even slowed down, and the losses sustained by the Japanese reduced their fleet from what had been at least a potential menace to mere nuisance level.'

As a result of their crushing defeat in the Battle of Leyte Gulf, and the likelihood of losing the war increasing daily as the Americans poured more men and materials into the Philippines, the Japanese began to launch furious air attacks on US shipping in Leyte Gulf, regardless of the cost to themselves. The *Kamikaze* suicide planes made their first appearance, often selecting PTs for attack so that there was a sharp increase at this time in casualties and the number of craft lost.

The main task of the PTs continued to be barge hunting. But during the weeks just before the US Army landings on the island of Mindoro on 15th

PTs shipping to Okinawa

Above: **President Truman congratulates Lieutenant-Commander Arthur Murray Preston after the awarding of the Medal of Honor**
Right: **Five-inch rockets were used by PTs in the Philippines**

December, they came into frequent contact with Japanese destroyers. A number of these ships were torpedoed, although it was not always possible to be certain of the extent of the damage caused. In one case however, there was no doubt of the outcome. On the night of 11th December two boats, PT 490 (Lieutenant John McElfresh USN) and PT 492 (Lieutenant Melvin Haines USNR) attacked a Japanese destroyer which had been sighted by radar off the west coast of Leyte. Two of their torpedoes hit with tremendous explosions and the destroyer, later confirmed as the 1,315-ton *Uzuki*, was seen to sink immediately, before being

aware even of the presence of the PT. This was the last action again: destroyers in the Leyte area.

By the end of December the Eighth Army had taken practical the entire island and the PTs mov up to a new base at Ormoc. Betwe then and March 1945, when the Eigh Army entered Cebu City, the boats squadrons 7, 12 and 25 had sunk mo than 140 barges, over sixty other sma craft loaded with troops and suppli with which the Japanese were tryi: to reinforce their positions, a: destroyed six aircraft.

At Mindoro meanwhile, the l invasion force which had landed 15th December was accompanied Squadrons 13 and 16, under the oper tional command of Lieutenant-Co mander Burt Davis USN. These boa gave valuable assistance again constant Japanese air attacks, brin ing down over twenty enemy plan

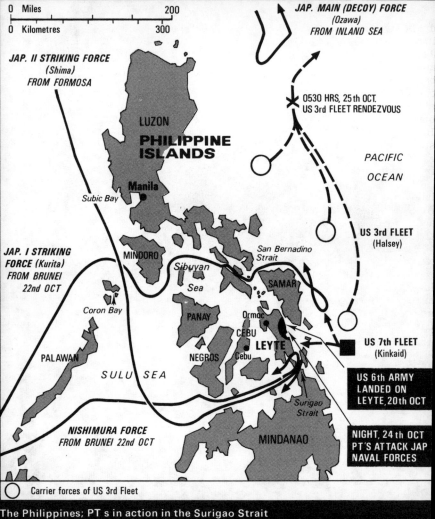

0 Miles 200

0 Kilometres 300

JAP. MAIN (DECOY) FORCE
(Ozawa)
FROM INLAND SEA

JAP. II STRIKING FORCE
(Shima)
FROM FORMOSA

LUZON

**PHILIPPINE
ISLANDS**

0530 HRS, 25th OCT.
US 3rd FLEET RENDEZVOUS

PACIFIC
OCEAN

Manila

Subic Bay

US 3rd FLEET
(Halsey)

JAP. I STRIKING
FORCE (Kurita)
FROM BRUNEI
22nd OCT

MINDORO

Sibuyan
Sea

San Bernadino
Strait

SAMAR

Coron Bay

PANAY

Ormoc

US 7th FLEET
(Kinkaid)

CEBU

LEYTE

Cebu

US 6th ARMY
LANDED ON
LEYTE, 20th OCT

PALAWAN

NEGROS

SULU SEA

Surigao
Strait

NIGHT, 24th OCT
PT'S ATTACK JAP
NAVAL FORCES

NISHIMURA FORCE
FROM BRUNEI 22nd OCT

MINDANAO

○ Carrier forces of US 3rd Fleet

The Philippines; PT s in action in the Surigao Strait

during the first few days of the landing. And when on 26th December the Japanese sent a battleship, a cruiser and six destroyers to carry out a naval bombardment of the American positions on Mindoro, the PTs helped US aircraft in driving off the enemy force – one boat, PT 233 (Lieutenant [jg] Harry Griffin Jr USN), being responsible for sinking the 2,100-ton destroyer *Kiyoshimo*, amongst the most powerful in the Japanese Navy.

In January, continuing their island-hopping strategy, the US Sixth Army launched a major assault against Luzon, the most northerly of the larger Philippine islands. The PTs again played an important part, carrying out diversionary attacks, escorting the landing parties, and landing scouts and raiders behind enemy lines. Squadrons 28 and 36, under the tactical command of Lieutenant-Commander Francis Tappaan USNR, took part in this operation, helped in the early stages by Squadrons 8, 24 and 25. Amongst these were boats made available as a result of the ending of the New Guinea campaign. The number of PT squadrons operating in the Philippines was increased to twenty, with Mindoro established as the principal repair and staging base.

Patrols from Mindoro continued until April. Much of the work of the PTs was in ferreting out small enemy craft hiding amongst the many bays and inlets and which no longer dared to venture into the open sea. One of the best hunting grounds proved to be Coron Bay, southeast of Mindoro. But the PTs by no means had everything their own way. Apart from frequent air attacks, both while at base and out to sea, they had to cope with storms and typhoons. Bases were often flooded out or reduced to seas of mud.

With virtually no navy left with which to fight, the Japanese at this time introduced the *Shinyo* suicide boats – simply small motor boats loaded with explosives which were intended to be piloted by one man against Allied ships. It became one of the main tasks of the PTs to locate and destroy these craft in their hideouts amongst the islands before they could be used. So successful were the PTs that there is no record of any ships being sunk or even damaged by the *Shinyo* boats, even though they were introduced in very large numbers.

The reopening of Subic Bay as an American naval base at the end of January led the way to the final drive to liberate Manila. The first Allied craft to enter Manila Bay since the American withdrawal in May 1942 were PTs – boats of Squadrons 21 and 27. And it was in another PT, 373, that General MacArthur returned to Corregidor on 2nd March 1945, nearly three years from the day he had left the Rock in PT 41 on 11th March 1942.

Throughout March and April the PTs continued to work with army units in liberating the smaller Philippine islands. But the fighting had now passed its peak. In the face of American air and sea superiority, the central Philippines had become a vast trap for the once victorious Japanese. Their remaining garrisons had to choose between surrender or annihilation.

Meanwhile, the American and Australian forces now turned their attention to Borneo. Landings were made during May, June and July at the great oil port of Balikpapan. PTs led the way to sink the Japanese suicide boats which still posed a threat and to strafe enemy shore installations. The final area of operations for PTs in the Pacific was to be Okinawa. But it was shortly after the first boats arrived there in August that hostilities ceased with Japan's surrender.

There were twenty-five PT squadrons in commission in the Pacific at that time. The majority of the boats were defective, with broken frames and keels and dry rot even apart from battle damage. But they had played their part, contributing greatly to final victory.

The final
Arakan campaign

The events in Europe and the Pacific in 1944 tended to overshadow the 'forgotten war' that was taking place in Southeast Asia, in which British and Empire forces under Admiral Lord Louis Mountbatten ought to hold back far greater numbers of Japanese on the very doorstep of India. But there were no dramatic victories with which to engage the world's attention. It was a low, arduous struggle, fought under appalling jungle conditions and with the Allies continually on the defensive. With the Japanese in control of almost the entire eastern coastline of the Indian Ocean, from Java, Sumatra, Malaya, and up to Burma, Allied efforts to take the offensive had from the start centred on Burma's Arakan coast, with the objective of capturing the Japanese stronghold at Akyab. The first Arakan campaign had begun in September 1942, in which MLs based at Chittagong were virtually the only light naval forces available, supporting the Fourteenth Army by making

Modified Fairmile D with two 6-pounders

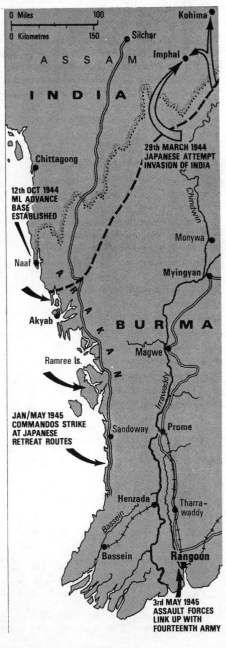

0 Miles 100
0 Kilometres 150

Kohima

Silchar

A S S A M

Imphal

I N D I A

Chittagong

29th MARCH 1944
JAPANESE ATTEMPT
INVASION OF INDIA

12th OCT 1944
ML ADVANCE
BASE
ESTABLISHED

Chindwin

Naaf

Monywa

Myingyan

B U R M A

Akyab

Magwe

Ramree Is.

Irrawaddy

JAN/MAY 1945
COMMANDOS STRIKE
AT JAPANESE
RETREAT ROUTES

Sandoway

Prome

Henzada

Tharra-
waddy

Bassein

Bassein

Rangoon

3rd MAY 1945
ASSAULT FORCES
LINK UP WITH
FOURTEENTH ARMY

Operations in Western Burma;
1944-spring 1945

numerous offshore raids. But without
sufficient reserves, the campaign
failed. By February 1943 the Allied
forces had been pushed back to their
original positions.

Following the appointment of Lord
Mountbatten as Supreme Allied Com
mander, Southeast Asia, in August
1943, a major assault in northern
Sumatra was planned. But with the
preparations then being made for the
invasions of Normandy and Southern
France, there were just not sufficient
forces available of, particularly, the
landing craft and small boats neces
sary to transport troops and supplies.
And so as a more modest alternative
it was decided to renew the attack on
Arakan, planned to coincide with a
Chinese offensive in northern Burma.

Only two MTB flotillas were opera
tional at this time, the 16th and 17th
based at Madras and Trincomalee and
operated by the Royal Indian Navy.
They comprised twenty-two Higgins
boats, transferred from the United
States under lend-lease. There were
constant maintenance difficulties
however, with few spare parts avail
able, and by May 1944 the boats had
deteriorated to such an extent that
they had to be scrapped. All that
remained were a few MLs, manned by
men of the British, Indian, Burmese
and South African navies.

During the first three months of 194
these craft patrolled the Arakan
coast in search of enemy vessels and
did what they could to support the
army's second Arakan campaign
which had started the previous
December. They landed parties of
Commandos and agents behind enemy
lines and raided coastal installations.
But they found few targets, since the
Japanese were able to move their
seaborne traffic through the maze of
inland waterways that were so much
a feature of the coastal region.

This campaign ended in April, with
the breaking of the monsoon and with
the Fourteenth Army having to turn
its attention to the north where the
Japanese had launched a maj

Above: Motor launches on their way to bombard Japanese shore defences on the Arakan coast. *Below:* Vosper's 1943 experimental prototype came too late to be used as an MTB class in the war, and was completed as an MGB

Wartime experience led to new propeller designs

attempt to invade India through Assam. It was not until the end of the year, after the Fourteenth Army had surprised the enemy by fighting through the monsoon period and at last turned the tide of battle against them, that the third and final Arakan campaign was launched.

By this time, British naval and air forces in the Indian Ocean had been considerably increased as the blockade of Japan tightened. Coastal Forces had also been expanded, with Commander R R W Ashby DSC, RNVR, the man who had made the trek from Hong Kong through China to Rangoon in 1942 and gone on to fight in MTBs in home and Mediterranean waters, appointed Senior Officer, Arakan Coastal Forces. It was off the Burmese coast that the final small boat fighting of the war took place.

Operating from a main base at Chittagong, the MLs had to cover a 400-mile stretch of enemy coastline as far south as the Bassein River. Their tasks included patrols against enemy supply vessels, attacks on ports and coastal installations, and in general helping the Army fighting in the north by holding down as many enemy troops as possible in coastal defence.

The craft allocated to Ashby were 36th, 37th, 49th, 55th, 56th and 57th flotillas of Fairmile MLs, the 146th and 147th HDML flotillas, the headquarters ship *Kedah* and maintenance ship *Barracuda*, and several small gasoline and water tenders. The MLs were formidably armed with a 3-pounder forward, single Oerlikon midships, 40mm Bofors aft, a twin Bren on the bridge, and two depth charges; many of them also mounted a 3-inch mortar aft. Except that they were 'B'-type Fairmiles instead of the 'D'-type, they were to all intents and purposes motor gunboats.

In the autumn of 1944 an advance base was established further down the Arakan coast at Naaf, and major operations started on 12th October, as soon as the monsoon season ended. Frequent sweeps were made along the entire coast, and although few enemy craft were encountered during the period until the end of the year, the presence of the MLs forced the Japanese to move their coastal supplies by the more arduous inland routes. They also took part in a number of successful Commando raids behind enemy lines.

The assault on Akyab which was one of the main objectives of the campaign was planned to take place in February. But at the end of December it was learned that the Japanese were already preparing to evacuate the port, prior to a general withdrawal southwards. The plan was brought forward, but when the first Commando brigade landed northwest of Akyab Island on 3rd January, the enemy had already left. The problem now was to cut off the Japanese forces retreating down the coast.

A series of Commando landings were made at points along the coast from where strikes could be made inland to the coastal road which was the enemy's main escape route. At the same time, the MLs were given the task of hunting down enemy craft carrying the retreating troops through the maze of inland waterways and jungle swamps.

These activities lasted until well into June, increasing after the liberation of Rangoon on 3rd May when MLs making their way up the Rangoon river with other assault forces made contact with the Fourteenth Army which had fought its way down central Burma. Again the Japanese had evacuated the port some days earlier. They had in fact abandoned their whole position in the Irrawaddy delta. But although lacking food and supplies because of the coastal blockade and in a state of complete disorganisation, some 100,000 trained Japanese troops still remained scattered throughout the region. In spite of facing defeat, they fought back with suicidal tenacity which made it no easy task for the MLs hunting them along the inland waterways.

Appalling weather conditions added to the difficulties especially after the rains began. The MLs were continually running aground – one grounded thirty-two times in nine days. And other hazards came from the booby-traps left behind by the retreating enemy. In many of the operations carried out against enemy barges, the MLs co-operated with Burmese living in the villages dotted along the river banks. The natives would give warning of approaching enemy craft by sounding gongs which reverberated through the dense jungle. The MLs would then move out from their hidden positions to intercept. Any Japanese troops who escaped the resulting engagement received short shrift at the hands of the Burmese, armed with spears and long-handled knives.

Few of the Japanese ever surrendered. In one report by a flotilla commander, Lieutenant-Commander John Wise DSC, RNVR, he stated: 'The courage or blind animal-like tenacity with which the enemy pressed on into the heavy and con centrated fire of our boats, even after his vessels had burst into flames, was a most sickening experience to watch In one case, one of the enemy returned to his beached vessel and, surrounded by flames, attempted to get his forward gun into action. Each boat was estimated to have carried ten or more Japanese. Of those who escaped destruction in their vessels, many were shot in the river or on the bank of the river.'

In that particular action, some enemy shells had landed in a riverside village, setting it on fire. However, as Wise wrote: 'the villagers seemed to think the night's entertainment was well worth it. They assured the ML they were perfectly all right and no one had been hurt. They set off with their spears to round up any Japanese who had got ashore.'

By the end of May the whole delta region had been cleared of enemy craft and only a few scattered Japanese troops were left on foot. During th

1968 Vosper-Thornycroft 60-knot missile-carrying fast patrol boat

ight months of the campaign, the
ILs had sunk thirty-one armed
anding craft, six motor gunboats, and
ixty-six smaller craft carrying
apanese troops. Their own losses had
een one ML, blown up after hitting a
aine.

Patrols continued until mid-June,
hen the heavy rains and flooding
aade the waterways unnavigable.
'ogether with other naval units, the
ILs began to make preparations for
ssaults on the Malay Peninsula. But
ae Japanese surrender came before
his operation had started.

A major reason for the effectiveness
f small fighting craft such as PTs,
ILs and MTBs in Southeast Asia and
ae Pacific was the lack of any suitable
apanese craft with which they could
e combated in coastal waters. It
ointed to the vital role that such
oats had to play in any conflict – a
.ct that was not readily appreciated
/ the major powers before the war
at which was certainly evident by the
ad of it. The Royal Navy, for instance,

from an ill-prepared beginning of only
twenty-four MTBs and MA/SBs in
1939, had built up a fleet of more than
1,600 small fighting craft by 1945. They
were highly effective against German
coastal convoys and in Commando
raids such as that on St Nazaire. But
probably their greatest value was in
counter attacking their German
motor torpedo boat equivalent, the
Schnellboote. Without them, British
merchant shipping would have suffered
far more grievously.

Since it was only in British home
waters and the Mediterranean that
similar opposing craft came up against
one another, in view of the neglect by
the Japanese to build MTBs, it is only
in these areas that any effective
comparison can be made.

British small boat losses during
the war totalled 223 – 115 MTBs, 28
MGBs, 79 MLs and 1 SGB. German and
Italian warship losses credited to

Missile-carrying FPB at practice

Coastal Forces totalled 70 ships, including 1 cruiser, 5 torpedo-boats, 1 armed merchant raider and 1 submarine. Of the remainder, most were German S-boats and R-boats and Italian MAS-boats. In addition, about 40 merchant ships were sunk by Coastal Forces in home waters, and some 100 merchant ships, including barge-type craft of small tonnage, in the Mediterranean (a number of them by American PTs).

The Germans lost 146 S-boats and 163 R-boats during the war, out of 244 and 326 respectively which were brought into operational service. (Of the 41 MAS-boats captured by the Germans after Italy's surrender and used as S-boats, 24 were destroyed; of the remaining 103 Italian MAS-boats in service during the war, 50 were destroyed, 20 scuttled, and the rest either taken over by the Allies or allowed to remain in Italian hands.) British Commonwealth warship losses

Advanced FPB design of 1970

credited to S-boats amounted to 4 ships, including 2 cruisers and destroyers. Merchant ships sunk b S-boats in all waters totalled 99, bu their tonnage, about 230,000 tons, wa nearly twice that of the 140 merchan craft sunk by British Coastal Force

What emerges from these figures and they can only be regarded a estimates for it was sometime impossible to tell whether a ship ha been sunk by mine or torpedo – is tha the German S-boats were overa more successful than the MTBs agains merchant shipping, while the MTE and MGBs were more successful whe it came to a straight encounter wit S-boats, But this had to be viewe against the greater number targets – in the way of British coast shipping – that were available to th Germans. British convoys average some forty ships, often escorted by n more than a couple of destroyers an a few MLs, whereas German convoy usually comprised no more than s merchant ships, with invariably

least a similar number of escorts.

By the very nature and geographical position of the war in the Pacific, America followed a policy of amphibious warfare from the very start. Britain was slower to do so, but it was when she did, after Dunkirk, that small boats came increasingly into their own. Command of enemy coastal waters became as important as defending those at home, and what began as limited Commando raids eventually evolved into full-scale invasions such as those in North Africa, Sicily, Italy, and finally the greatest of them all in Normandy.

After the war, Coastal Forces suffered much the same fate as they had in 1918. Boats were broken up or sold, building and research programmes cancelled, and once again it was left primarily to private companies to continue what limited small boat development there was. Only in 1954 did the Admiralty order two Fast Patrol Boats, as the MTBs were then reclassified, from the combined

Vosper-Thornycroft Group. These were the Brave class boats – *Brave Borderer* and *Brave Swordsman* – ninety-six-foot, 50-knot craft, armed with electrically operated 40mm Bofors guns and four 21-inch torpedoes carried in side-launching chutes, of which the Group had already sold a number to other countries.

In the meantime, a private venture programme by the Group had led to an even more sophisticated gas-turbine FPB, mounting various types of guided missile. Of the eighteen boats of this type in service or under construction in 1968, sixteen were for foreign navies – those of Denmark, Malaya, Libya, Greece and Brunei – and only two on order for the Royal Navy.

Other countries, and in particular the United States, have also made progress in the development of missile-carrying FPBs. A recent feature has been the introduction of hydrofoils to these craft – a stilt-like device for lifting the hulls clear of the water in order to reduce drag, thereby increasing speed. Two types of hydrofoil gunboats currently being developed for the US Navy by Boeing and Grumman are likely to see service in a number of European navies as well. And development work on hydrofoil craft is also taking place in the Soviet Union, Italy, Japan, Germany and Canada, with obvious military applications. Britain has tended to neglect hydrofoils, favouring instead the development of an entirely new type of craft, the hovercraft, using the air cushion principle as a means of avoiding any contact at all with the surface and thus making very great speeds possible.

In a generation which has seen guided missiles of various types threaten so many conventional weapons with obsolescence, the speed and smallness of target of torpedo-gunboats will ensure a place for them as part of any defence of coastal waters, just as the same characteristics proved their value in the Second World War.

Bibliography

We Fought them in Gunboats Lt Cdr Robert Hichens, RNVR (Michael Joseph, London)

The Little Ships Gordon Holman (Hodder & Stoughton, London)

Flag 4 Dudley Pope (William Kimber, London)

The Battle of the Narrow Seas Lt Cdr Peter Scott, RNVR (Country Life, London)

The Navy at War 1939–1945 Captain S W Roskill, RN (Collins, London)

White Ensign, the British Navy at War 1939–1945 Captain S W Roskill, RN (US Naval Institute, Annapolis)

At Close Quarters Captain Robert J Bulkley Jr, USNR (Government Printing Office, Washington)

Alarm – Schnellboote Jan Mayen (Gerhard Stalling Verlag, Oldenberg)

The War at Sea: UK Military History 3 volumes Captain S W Roskill, RN (HMSO, London)

The History of United States Naval Operations in World War II Professor S E Morison (Little, Brown & Co, Boston. Oxford, London)

The RNVR J L Kerr and W Granville (Harrap, London)

The Watery Maze – The Story of Combined Operations Sir B Fergusson (Collins, London)